Runway To Real Life Model's Journey

Runway To Real Life Model's Journey

Rafeal Mechlore

UNIEK ENTERPRISES

CONTENTS

INDEX

Chapter Six: Real World Integration

Chapter Seven: The Impact of Diversity

Chapter Eight: The Pursuit of Passion

Introduction

In the enrapturing domain of design, where craftsmanship meets trade, models stand at the cutting edge of a groundbreaking industry that is everlastingly developing. The runway, with its amazing lights and excessive plans, fills in as the platform for these charming excursions that mesh dreams into the real world. In the background, underneath the excitement, lies the untold story of a model's change from a youngster visionary into a genuine symbol of style and elegance.

This excursion isn't just about swaggering down catwalks in the most recent high fashion or gracing the pages of lustrous magazines. It's a significant odyssey, a soul changing experience, where hopefuls are changed into cleaned experts who explore a multifaceted world that sways among goal and reality. This complicated and diverse development from runway to genuine is an embroidery woven sincerely, flexibility, and, frequently, a hint of luck.

Demonstrating, as an occupation, is many times glamorized and perplexing, covered in persona and charm. However, underneath the surface, the universe of demonstrating is a requesting one, requiring an unprecedented mix of excellence, beauty, and business intuition. A world has progressed significantly, developing from the time of supermodels to the period of powerhouses. Furthermore, through this change, models have become something beyond strolling holders; they have become narrators, business people, and powerhouses by their own doing.

The excursion of a model, from the sparkling catwalks to the roads of day to day existence, includes the preliminaries and wins of self-improvement, proficient turn of events, and cultural change. A journey interweaves with more extensive social movements, mirroring the developing view of excellence, personality, and validness. In this investigation of a model's excursion, we dive into the significant transformation that happens as they cross the runway to the real world. The accompanying words will take you on an entrancing visit through the stunning universe of style displaying, where the spotlight isn't simply on the garments yet in addition on the lives, dreams, and goals of the actual models.

Each model starts as a fresh start, a work of crude potential. The excursion starts when a fantasy is touched off, a flash of desire that drives them into the universe of projecting calls, tryouts, and portfolio building. The runway calls, and models answer that call with a blend of energy, ability, and, frequently, an equivalent proportion of vulnerability.

The mission to turn into a model is a rollercoaster ride of disclosure and self-personality. Hopeful models leave on a thorough self-assessment, stripping back the layers to find who they genuinely are and the way in which they wish to be seen by the world. This course of self-disclosure isn't just an individual arousing yet an expert objective, as models should characterize their remarkable allure in an industry that blossoms with uniqueness.

A model's process starts with the projecting calls, an underlying openness to the merciless truth of the business. The projecting room, with its unforgiving lighting, examining eyes, and the frequently fierce excusal of hopefuls, is a position of the two dreams and disillusionments. Dismissal is an integral part of this world, where just the strong get by. Models should defy dismissal head-on, gaining from it, developing through it, and arising more grounded with each insight.

In the midst of the difficulties of projecting calls, models should likewise explore the sensitive harmony among certainty and modesty. The business requests trust in one's capacities and appearance, yet lowliness to acknowledge study, adjust, and advance. Finding some kind of harmony is a work of art in itself, as models discover that self-assuredness, not pomposity, is the way to establishing a long term connection.

In any case, the runway venture isn't only about the shallow; it requires a scholarly keenness. Models should get a handle on the language of design, grasp drifts, and figure out the creativity behind each fasten and crease. They change into something beyond strolling life sized models; they become epicureans of configuration, pushing for their own innovative vision while teaming up consistently with planners and picture takers to rejuvenate that vision.

The runway is where a model's genuineness, balance, and beauty sparkle the most splendid. Strolling down the runway is a presentation, a work of art that requires accuracy and polish. Finding some kind of harmony between saying something and exemplifying the substance of a fashioner's creation is the model's test. Furthermore, as they walk that runway, they rejuvenate those manifestations, changing texture into dream.

As they ace the art of strolling, models likewise become amazing at presenting. Their bodies become devices of imaginative articulation, fit for conveying a large number of feelings and stories with the subtlest of motions. Through photography, they catch minutes in time, freeze casings of magnificence and style that rise above the limits of the design world. The change from a runway walker to a visual dream is a demonstration of the flexibility and versatility that displaying requests.

The runway venture, in any case, isn't just about individual development; it is tied in with embracing variety and destroying generalizations. The style business, long evaluated for its restricted portrayal of excellence, is going through a momentous change. Models are currently pushing limits, breaking generalizations, and expanding the range of excellence that is commended. As the business develops, the runway venture turns into an instrument of progress, where models advocate for inclusivity, challenge customary thoughts of magnificence, and embrace the force of variety.

This change isn't simply a momentary pattern; a development perceives the magnificence in the entirety of its shifted structures. Models are at the very front of this social shift, utilizing their foundation to advocate for change, separate boundaries, and rethink excellence guidelines. As they walk the runway, they convey with them the voices of the unheard and the fantasies of the individuals who set out to appear as something else.

The excursion from runway to genuine is likewise a trial of physical and mental perseverance. The glamour and excitement of the runway frequently hide the requesting and thorough timetables that models should stick to. Extended periods of time, steady travel, and the strain to keep up with flawless actual shape are a vital part of the calling. Models should figure out how to adjust taking care of oneself and profession requests, an errand that can be truly and intellectually burdening.

The strain to adjust to cultural norms of excellence can negatively affect a model's confidence. The runway venture isn't without its difficulties, as models might wrestle with issues of self-perception, self-uncertainty, and personality. The consistent investigation of one's appearance, both by industry experts and general society, can overpower. However, inside these difficulties models find their internal strength, flexibility, and the force of self-acknowledgment.

The runway venture is likewise a journey of self-articulation. Models, through their own style and uniqueness, make a personality that separates them. They change into style symbols, impacting patterns and characterizing design developments. This individual style frequently rises above the runway, saturating the genuine existences of their admirers who seek models for motivation and direction on the most proficient method to dress, how to convey themselves, and how to be proudly themselves.

Models are not generally restricted to the runway and style magazines. In the period of online entertainment, they have become persuasive figures who shape design as well as the more extensive culture. Their internet based presence is a material for narrating, where they can share their qualities, encounters, and interests. In this advanced age, models are not simply models; they are content makers, forces to be reckoned with, and business visionaries who have the ability to shape general assessment and catalyze social change.

The runway venture is certainly not a single one. Models frequently wind up working in different groups, teaming up with photographic artists, fashioners, cosmetics craftsmen, and beauticians. This cooperative soul is a fundamental piece of the business, where the combination of imaginative energies brings about shocking show-stoppers. As models progress in their vocations, they become people as well as fundamental gear-teeth in a perfectly tuned symphony, each contributing their one of a kind gifts to an aggregate vision.

Behind each effective model, there is an emotionally supportive network of family, companions, and coaches who energize and direct them. These connections assume a significant part in a model's excursion, giving the profound and proficient help expected to climate the difficulties and praise the victories. The change from runway to genuine is, in numerous ways, an aggregate exertion, with models depending on their networks to assist them with exploring the unusual territory of the business.

While the runway venture has its own novel arrangement of difficulties, it additionally offers momentous open doors for movement and openness to assorted societies. Models become worldwide residents, streaming off to design capitals like Paris, Milan, New York, and Tokyo. This openness improves their lives, expands their perspectives, and upgrades their social mindfulness. Models exhibit design as well as become ministers of social trade, bringing the world nearer through the general language of style.

The runway venture is however much about offering back as it could be tied in with getting. Many models channel their prosperity into magnanimous undertakings, utilizing their foundation to bring issues to light and support different causes. They become advocates for social change, utilizing their voices to resolve issues like natural manageability, orientation fairness, and civil rights. The runway, when a position of imagination, changes into a phase for activism, where models work to make a superior world both inside and past the design business.

1. **The Allure of the Runway**

   The runway, an apparently interminable stretch of sparkling white, is the core of the design business. A phase where dreams are understood, and dreams rejuvenated, it is a position of charm and charm. In the realm of style, the runway is much the same as a theater where pieces of clothing change into craftsmanship, models become residing figures, and creators' dreams manifest into the real world.

   The runway's charm rises above simple genuineness; it is a domain where the phenomenal and the ordinary join, where the significant and the shallow coincide. Its attractive allure lies an option for its to embody the whole design story inside a couple of transient minutes. A fleeting world lights energy, incites interest, and welcomes the crowd to step into the domain of dreams and wants.

   The runway isn't only a stage for introducing clothing; it is a phase for the exhibition of style, workmanship, and culture. Each runway show is a painstakingly arranged presentation that wires music, lighting, development, and design to make a display that is both tastefully stunning and genuinely mixing. This combination of components raises the runway from a simple stage to an enrapturing theater of design.

   As the lights faint and the crowd quiets in expectation, the runway changes into an entryway to an alternate aspect. The charm starts with the main model's appearance. With each step, the model recounts to a story through development, stance, and articulation. The article of clothing, an expansion of the model's persona, talks about the architect's vision and the wearer's character.

The charm of the runway lies in its capacity to move the crowd to an existence where time eases back, and reality obscures. The crowd turns out to be important for a selective, transient experience, where they witness the summit of long periods of plan, craftsmanship, and imaginative vision in no time flat. The runway, with its carefully arranged plans and coordinated movement, makes an environment of suspended reality, where the phenomenal turns into the standard.

The appeal of the runway is additionally well established in its ability to exhibit the always developing idea of magnificence. Models, with their novel elements, become the living materials whereupon architects paint their dreams. The runway is a demonstration of the festival of variety, where models of all foundations, shapes, sizes, and sexes march their singular excellence and elegance. It is a domain where the customary principles of magnificence are tested, where validness rules, and where each model turns into a symbol of self-articulation.

The runway is a stage for visual narrating, where style stories are woven through every outfit. With each step, models describe stories of tastefulness, resistance, sentimentality, and futurism. The runway is an embroidery of feelings, temperaments, and sensations, mirroring the steadily changing outlook of the style business. It fills in as a mirror to society, catching the social and cultural movements existing apart from everything else.

The appeal of the runway isn't restricted to the pieces of clothing and the models alone. It reaches out to the behind the stage disorder, where fashioners, cosmetics craftsmen, hair specialists, and beauticians work energetically to guarantee that everything about faultless. It is in the in the background show that the crowd can witness the energy, commitment, and craftsmanship that go into making the runway sorcery.

The runway's appeal is additionally elevated by the actual crowd. Onlookers from varying backgrounds, decorated in their best clothing, meet up to observe the scene. The runway rises above financial, social, and generational limits, making a space where variety and inclusivity are trendy expressions as well as unmistakable real factors. As the crowd sits down, the runway turns into a microcosm of the world, where alternate points of view join, and where style fills in as a widespread language that rises above words.

The appeal of the runway is additionally in its capacity to start precedents and rethink style. It is where originators face challenges, push limits, and stir things up. What shows up on the runway today frequently turns into the design of tomorrow, affecting what we wear as well as how we see and articulate our thoughts. The runway is a favorable place for development and imagination, a domain where the limits of style are constantly extended and re-imagined.

The runway's charm isn't limited by geology or culture; it is an all inclusive peculiarity. Whether in the style capitals of Paris, Milan, New York, or the blossoming scenes of developing business sectors, the runway enamors and moves. Every area carries its one of a kind flavor and translation to the runway, mirroring the neighborhood style, customs, and impacts. The appeal of the runway is essentially as different as the design world itself.

The appeal of the runway stretches out past the design business. It resounds with a more extensive crowd, charming the people who may not be personally associated with the universe of design. Runway shows are live exhibitions that join workmanship, culture, and amusement. They give a tangible encounter that draws in the crowd on various levels, making it a fascination for lovers of plan, music, movement, from there, the sky is the limit.

The appeal of the runway additionally lies in its authentic importance. The runway has seen the development of style over hundreds of years, mirroring the evolving standards, values, and advances of society. From the lavish ensembles of the Renaissance to the smooth and moderate plans of the cutting edge period, the runway is a living gallery of design's set of experiences. It permits us to follow the strings of fashion development, offering bits of knowledge into the socio-social setting of every time.

The appeal of the runway isn't restricted to the universe of high style. Streetwear and metropolitan design have cut their own specialty on the runway, overcoming any issues between regular style and high style. The runway has turned into where subcultures, nonconformities, and underground developments track down articulation, obscuring the lines among style and craftsmanship. It is a space where insubordination, development, and self-articulation are praised.

The appeal of the runway stretches out to the domain of big name. Runway appearances by superstars, frequently as a team with originators, act as a converging of diversion and style. These minutes earn consideration, obscuring the lines among Hollywood and the runway, making a combination of businesses that dazzles the public's creative mind. The runway has turned into where acclaim and design meet, affecting patterns and motivating fans around the world.

The appeal of the runway is likewise intently attached to the idea of extravagance. Top of the line style brands use the runway as a stage to feature their most restrictive and cutting edge manifestations. These runway shows are not just about apparel; they are about brand character, selectiveness, and craftsmanship. The runway is a space where extravagance and craftsmanship join, permitting brands to recount to a story that rises above material belongings.

The appeal of the runway is established in its persona. It is an existence where dream meets reality, where planners' fantasies show some major signs of life, and where models change into residing figures. The runway is where the common is raised to the exceptional, where the unremarkable is transformed into display, and where design becomes craftsmanship. It is a domain where magnificence is commended in the entirety of its structures, where variety rules, and where genuineness is valued.

The appeal of the runway isn't static; it is consistently developing. The style business, with its always evolving scene, continually rethinks the charm of the runway. Runway shows adjust to the computerized age, embracing livestreams and web-based entertainment to contact a worldwide crowd. The runway, once restricted to tip top occasions, has become available to design fans around the world, extending its appeal and impact.

The charm of the runway is a demonstration of the getting through force of design. It is an existence where innovativeness exceeds all logical limitations, where self-articulation is commended, and where development flourishes. The runway is where the fantasies of planners, models, and form devotees unite, making a scene that rises above overall setting.

In the realm of style, the charm of the runway is a persevering through interest that proceeds to enthrall and move. It is an existence where magnificence, style, and self-articulation meet up to make a spellbinding story. The runway isn't simply a phase; it is a domain where dreams are made, where craftsmanship is praised, and where the enchantment of style unfurls in the entirety of its magnificence. It is where the uncommon becomes conventional, and where the charm of the runway allures us to participate in its captivating dance of style and beauty.

2. **The Realities Behind the Glamour**

In the realm of design, where style and marvelousness become the dominant focal point, being lured by the charm of the runway and the lustrous pages of design magazines is simple. Design models, specifically, are frequently viewed as images of magnificence, style, and flawlessness. They beauty the fronts of magazines, stroll down lofty runways, and appear to lead experiences that the greater part of us can merely fantasize about. Notwithstanding, reality in the background uncovers that the marvelous façade frequently covers a universe of difficulties, penances, and intricacies that models explore on their excursion to progress.

The pathway to turning into an effective style model is everything except direct. While it might give the idea that these people are simply brought into the world with natural magnificence and elegance, actually their process is cleared with difficult work, versatility, and, on occasion, a dash of good fortune. To comprehend the intricacies of this industry, it's pivotal to look past the surface and recognize the innate difficulties that design models face.

The street to turning into a model starts with projecting calls and tryouts. These are the underlying advances that hopeful models should take, and they can unbelievably dismay. In the realm of projecting calls, the initial feeling is much of the time the main impression, and the opposition is wild. Models, no matter what their experience or potential, may confront dismissal over and over before they get their most memorable break.

This course of tryouts isn't just about displaying one's actual properties; it's tied in with depicting character and character. Models should persuade projecting specialists and originators that they have the right demeanor and presence to exemplify the brand's vision. Certainty and magnetism, alongside a solid comprehension of design and style, are fundamental for establishing a long term connection during these tryouts.

The excursion from tryouts to runway shows isn't just about actual change yet additionally about self-improvement. Models should go through a course of self-revelation and self-definition. This is an essential piece of their excursion in light of the fact that, in a world that blossoms with uniqueness and distinction, models should comprehend what their identity and separates them.

In the design business, models frequently face analysis and examination about their appearance and body. These studies can be steady and, now and again, horrible. The strain to adjust to customary guidelines of excellence can negatively affect a model's confidence, prompting issues connected with self-perception and self-question. The truth behind the allure is that even in an industry that celebrates excellence, the meaning of magnificence can be uncommonly limited, and this limitation can be crippling for models who don't fit the shape.

Another unmistakable reality that models face is the transient idea of their vocations. Displaying is certainly not a long lasting calling generally speaking. The typical displaying vocation can be very short, frequently enduring a couple of years. Models should persistently adjust to the developing business scene and wrestle with the vulnerability of what comes next after their demonstrating vocation finishes up. They are in many cases passed on to address what they will progress into when the runway is at this point not their stage.

The requests of a demonstrating vocation are genuinely and intellectually burdening. Keeping a particular appearance and body is a continuous test. The business' severe guidelines imply that models should keep a particular weight and size, frequently requiring an exhausting routine of diet and exercise. For some's purposes, this strain can prompt unfortunate things to do and dietary problems, which represent an impressive gamble to both their physical and mental prosperity.

The style world's thorough timetables can overpower too. Models frequently get through extended periods of time, broad travel, and steady appearances at style occasions and shows. This way of life, while marvelous on a superficial level, can prompt weariness and burnout. The test of offsetting taking care of oneself with vocation requests is a ceaseless fight for models.

The runway might show up as a breathtaking universe of creator garments, however actually many models are frequently neglected or come up short on for their work. This issue of remuneration uniqueness, where a chosen handful top models procure significant sums while others battle to earn barely enough to get by, highlights the disparity present in the business. A few models face shady practices, like neglected gigs and unjustifiable working circumstances.

The assumptions put on models to be powerhouses and diplomats for brands reach out past the runway. With the ascent of virtual entertainment, models are supposed to develop an individual brand and have a critical web-based presence. Keeping a drawing in and cautiously organized online entertainment presence can be a regular work, adding to the tensions of a demonstrating vocation.

The design business isn't insusceptible to fundamental issues like segregation, provocation, and double-dealing. Models, similar to others in the business, may experience segregation in view of variables like race, orientation, and age. Provocation, as well, is a dreary reality for certain models, who might persevere through unseemly way of behaving from those in, strategic, influential places. The business has gone under examination for its absence of securities and emotionally supportive networks for models confronting such issues.

The idea of life span and professional stability is frequently tricky for models. Models are continually in quest for the following gig, as open positions are irregular and sporadic. While top models might appreciate critical achievement and monetary strength, by far most of models wrestle with the flimsiness of independent work, unsure pay, and holes between projects.

The charm of design week is a zenith second for models, yet it accompanies its own arrangement of difficulties. Runway shows are high-pressure occasions, with models expected to execute exact movement while keeping a ready and certain disposition. The high speed nature of these occasions can be both elating and depleting.

Displaying is likewise a field where age assumes a huge part. While the business has become more comprehensive as of late, ageism stays an unavoidable issue. Many models find their professions level as they become older, and just a limited handful appreciate life span in the business.

The extraordinary contest and drive for progress can in some cases lead to an absence of fellowship among models. The feeling of contest can establish a climate where models may not necessarily in all cases backing or post for each other, and this can compound sensations of detachment and frailty.

The demonstrating business has for quite some time been evaluated for its absence of variety and portrayal. By and large, the business maintained unbending excellence guidelines that inclined toward a restricted arrangement of highlights and body types. This absence of variety propagated hurtful generalizations as well as avoided people from underrepresented foundations. Models of variety, larger size models, and LGBTQ+ models have needed to challenge these standards and push for more comprehensive portrayal.

For every one of its difficulties, the charm of the runway is unquestionably strong. Design models encapsulate the optimistic soul of the business, addressing a definitive acknowledgment of excellence, style, and charm. Their presence on runways, in magazines, and via web-based entertainment keeps on spellbinding crowds, motivate originators, and set precedents. The universe of demonstrating is a complicated embroidery of desire, magnificence, and opportunity, and for some, the charm of the runway demonstrates powerful.

While the difficulties and real factors behind the marvelousness of the runway are irrefutable, it's memorable's fundamental that the business has additionally taken huge steps toward positive change. Variety and inclusivity are progressively celebrated, giving a stage to a more extensive scope of voices and viewpoints. Models are currently taking advantage of their leverage to advocate for positive change, both inside the design business and in the public eye at large.

The truth behind the charm of the runway advises us that each model is a person with their own battles and yearnings. Their processes are loaded up with ups and downs, difficulties and wins. As we keep on valuing the excellence and imaginativeness of style models, it is similarly critical to recognize and uphold them as they continued looking for a more comprehensive, fair, and different industry. The charm of the runway might be powerful, yet the genuine accounts of models make the style world really enrapturing and groundbreaking.

3. **Purpose and Scope of the Book**

In a quickly changing and progressively interconnected world, the journey to comprehend and explore the mind boggling elements of global relations has never been more fundamental. This book sets out on an excursion to investigate the unpredictable trap of worldwide governmental issues, discretion, and global participation, trying to give perusers an extensive and smart point of view on the complex domain of global relations.

The motivation behind this book is to reveal insight into the perplexing and frequently cryptic universe of worldwide relations. It expects to offer perusers a more profound comprehension of the powers, entertainers, and foundations that shape our worldwide scene, as well as the critical issues and difficulties that characterize the global stage in the 21st 100 years. By digging into the intricacies of worldwide relations, this book endeavors to furnish perusers with the information and bits of knowledge expected to draw in with and get a handle on the world's most major problems, from worldwide clash to monetary reliance, from environmental change to common freedoms.

The extent of this book is deliberately wide, incorporating a different cluster of points, ideas, and occasions that on the whole comprise the rich embroidery of global relations. It is intended to act as both an acquaintance for those new with the field and an asset for those looking for a more top to bottom comprehension of explicit issues or improvements. Through a multidisciplinary approach, this book tends to key subjects and areas of interest, offering perusers an extensive outline of the field of global relations.

At the core of this book is the acknowledgment that worldwide relations are not bound to the worries of policymakers, negotiators, or researchers alone; they are of crucial significance to every one of us. In our interconnected world, the choices made by pioneers and state run administrations in a single corner of the globe have extensive results, impacting economies, security, and the climate around the world. Consequently, it is critical for people from varying backgrounds to be educated and participated in the conversation regarding global relations, as it straightforwardly influences the personal satisfaction and the condition of the world we live in.

The book is coordinated into a few topical segments, each diving into key parts of worldwide relations. These segments give a guide to explore the complicated scene of worldwide governmental issues and strategy, offering an organized way to deal with fathoming the complex universe of global relations. The segments are as per the following:

Prologue to Global Relations: This segment sets the stage by presenting the central ideas and hypotheses that support the field of worldwide relations. It investigates the verifiable advancement of the discipline, key hypothetical points of view, and the different entertainers and elements that impact foreign relations.

Worldwide Legislative issues and Administration: Here, the book dives into the designs and components of worldwide administration, looking at establishments like the Unified Countries, territorial associations, and non-state entertainers that assume essential parts in forming global governmental issues. It additionally addresses the difficulties of worldwide administration, including issues of force, sway, and the effect of arising powers.

Struggle and Security: Struggle is a persevering through element of global relations, and this part investigates the different components of contention, from highway battles to psychological warfare and digital dangers. It likewise inspects the methodologies and systems for compromise and peacekeeping, and the advancing idea of human security.

Financial aspects and Globalization: During a time of monetary reliance, this segment looks at the multifaceted connection between worldwide financial aspects and worldwide governmental issues. Points covered incorporate exchange, money, advancement, and the job of global foundations like the World Exchange Association and the Worldwide Financial Asset.

Ecological and Transnational Issues: The worldwide difficulties within recent memory stretch out past boundaries. This part resolves basic transnational issues, for example, environmental change, pandemics, common liberties, and relocation. It investigates the job of global associations, arrangements, and compassionate endeavors in resolving these complicated issues.

Social Discretion and Delicate Power: In an undeniably interconnected world, the trading of thoughts, values, and culture assumes a huge part in molding global relations. This part explores the idea of delicate power and social tact, inspecting how countries project their impact through culture, media, and schooling.

The Eventual fate of Worldwide Relations: The last segment examines the eventual fate of global relations, taking into account arising patterns and difficulties in the field. It investigates the effect of mechanical headways, changes in worldwide power elements, and the advancing idea of contention and collaboration.

All through each part, the book tries to give a fair and nuanced point of view on complex issues, recognizing the different perspectives and approaches that shape the field of worldwide relations. It draws from verifiable occasions, contemporary contextual investigations, and a wide cluster of scholastic and strategy writing to offer perusers an extensive and exceptional comprehension of the worldwide scene.

The extent of this book stretches out past intellectual or hypothetical conversations. It is intended to be a significant asset for understudies, researchers, policymakers, and anyone with any interest in understanding the complex universe of worldwide relations. It energizes decisive reasoning, cultivates a feeling of worldwide citizenship, and outfits perusers with the information and experiences expected to participate in significant conversations and add to the aggregate exertion of tending to worldwide difficulties.

Notwithstanding its instructive reason, this book tries to be a reference guide for those looking to explore the intricacies of global relations in their own and proficient lives. Whether one is keen on figuring out the reasons for worldwide contentions, the complexities of global exchange, the elements of worldwide administration, or the ramifications of environmental change, this book offers a far reaching investigation of these points and that's just the beginning.

At last, the reason and extent of this book are established in the conviction that educated and drew in people are essential to encouraging a more serene, just, and feasible world. By digging into the real factors behind the fabulousness of global relations, we can more readily grasp the intricate powers that shape our reality and work by and large to address the squeezing worldwide difficulties within recent memory.

Chapter One

The Aspiring Models

In the charming and frequently confounding universe of style, hopeful models are the soul of the business. They are the visionaries who long to elegance the polished pages of magazines, swagger down the renowned runways, and become symbols of style and magnificence. These hopeful models set out on an extraordinary excursion, driven by their energy for design, their fantasies of self-articulation, and the craving to make an imprint on the steadily developing scene of the style business.

The goal to turn into a model is a fantasy that has lighted the hearts of innumerable people, paying little mind to mature, orientation, or foundation. For some, the excursion starts with a flash of desire, an interest with the universe of design, and a dream of themselves as the exemplification of style and beauty. In any case, the way from goal to acknowledgment is nowhere near clear and is weighed down with difficulties, self-improvement, and, now and again, snapshots of self-disclosure.

The initial step on the excursion of a hopeful model is much of the time the universe of projecting calls and tryouts. These underlying experiences are a basic commencement into the business, where models should gather their certainty, balance, and self-show abilities to establish a significant connection. The projecting room, frequently unmistakably lit and loaded up with investigating eyes, is a position of the two dreams and disillusionments. Hopeful models might encounter dismissal as often as possible, as contest is extraordinary, and just a limited handful are decided to push ahead.

The tryout cycle isn't exclusively about actual qualities; it is likewise a chance for models to convey their characters, their flexibility, and their capacity to squeeze into an originator's vision. Models must grandstand their certainty, show their novel appeal, and exhibit a profound comprehension of design and style. Inside these tryout minutes hopeful models make their most memorable strides towards the runway.

Exploring the universe of tryouts requires hopeful models to find some kind of harmony between self-assuredness and lowliness. Certainty is essential in an industry where confident people frequently stick out, however lowliness is similarly significant as models should acknowledge studies, gain from dismissal, and persistently adjust and develop.

Hopeful models find that these tryouts offer open doors as well as experiences into self-show. Each experience gives an opportunity to self-assessment, as models should investigate their assets and shortcomings, characterize their one of a kind allure, and refine their show abilities. Through these tryouts models leave on an excursion of self-revelation, as they figure out how to characterize themselves in an industry that blossoms with peculiarity.

The charm of the runway allures hopeful models and constrains them to endure through the difficulties of tryouts and projecting calls. The runway addresses the zenith of their fantasies, where they change into residing figures, epitomizing the inventive dreams of originators. Strolling down the runway isn't simply an actual execution yet a work of art in itself. It requires accuracy, balance, and elegance, as models should convey the substance of an originator's creation with each step.

The runway is where a hopeful model's rawness turns into a vehicle of imaginative articulation. Each development, each posture, and each signal should convey a story, inspire an inclination, and rejuvenate the creator's vision. This part of displaying involves a degree of preparing and discipline that stretches out past the underlying desires of many models. It requires a significant association with one's body and a commitment to consummating the craft of development.

Models likewise explore the fragile craft of presenting, where their bodies become instruments of narrating. Posturing for photos requests a comprehension of how to pass feelings and stories on through the subtlest motions and articulations. The change from runway walker to visual dream is a demonstration of the flexibility and versatility that displaying requests.

Be that as it may, the goal to turn into a model isn't just an excursion of outside change; it is likewise a significant odyssey of self-improvement and self-definition. The business frequently puts weighty accentuation on the actual parts of displaying, however the truth behind the fabulousness uncovers that hopeful models should likewise sharpen their inward characteristics. Certainty, flexibility, and versatility are characteristics that models should develop to flourish in the realm of design.

The desire to turn into a model is a demonstration of the persevering through charm of style and the widespread interest with excellence. Models, through their special elements, become living materials whereupon architects paint their dreams. The runway is a stage for commending variety, where models of all foundations, shapes, sizes, and sexual orientations march their singular excellence and elegance. It is a domain where the conventional principles of magnificence are tested, where realness is valued, and where models change into symbols of self-articulation.

The change from hopeful model to runway proficient is set apart by encounters of both victory and hardship. The hopeful models might experience snapshots of self-question, where the strain to adjust to limit guidelines of magnificence can prompt inquiries regarding self-esteem. They might wrestle with issues connected with self-perception and confidence, in an industry where actual appearance is of foremost significance.

The runway venture, with its physical and mental requests, expects models to find some kind of harmony between taking care of oneself and profession commitments. The breathtaking façade of the business may at times darken the cost it takes on models' prosperity. The actual afflictions, requesting timetables, and strain to keep up with perfect actual shape can be truly and intellectually burdening.

The quest for a displaying profession likewise presents the test of keeping up with one's credibility. In an industry that frequently centers around outer appearances, hopeful models should protect their inward characters, convictions, and values. Keeping up with one's genuineness is a fine harmony between adjusting to the necessities of the business and remaining consistent with one's very own convictions.

The runway venture is accentuated by snapshots of progress, where hopeful models should arrive at basic conclusions about their fates. The displaying profession, however frequently concise for the vast majority, outfits models with a special arrangement of abilities and encounters that can be applied in different fields. Choosing when to step off the runway and investigate new skylines is a critical decision that models should make.

As they change from hopeful models to experts, some decide to wander into different ways that mirror their developing advantages and desires. Many track down satisfaction in seeking after vocations as planners, cosmetics craftsmen, or beauticians, utilizing their insight into the business. Others leave on ventures in business, diversion, or charity, utilizing their leverage to have a beneficial outcome on society.

While hopeful models may at first be enamored by the style of the runway, the truth in the background uncovers that the excursion is nowhere near direct. It is set apart by snapshots of self-uncertainty, dismissal, and self-awareness. Be that as it may, the groundbreaking force of the runway venture lies in its ability to foster versatility, certainty, and flexibility in the people who seek after it.

The yearning to turn into a model isn't restricted by orientation, age, or foundation. A fantasy entices people from varying backgrounds, who set out to pursue their yearnings and embrace their uniqueness. The universe of style has developed to commend variety and inclusivity, and hopeful models keep on testing conventional standards, making the runway a more comprehensive and delegate stage.

The runway venture is a persevering through story, one that rises above ages and stays a demonstration of the immortal charm of design. Hopeful models exemplify the optimistic soul of the business, and their fantasies and yearnings keep on rousing ages to come. In the steadily developing universe of design, the goal to turn into a model remaining parts an image of magnificence, style, and self-articulation.

The yearning to turn into a model isn't simply an individual mission for excellence and acknowledgment; it is an impression of society's interest with design and its ability to change lives. The runway venture, with its one of a kind mix of excitement and reality, addresses the widespread yearning for self-articulation, independence, and the acknowledgment of dreams. Trying models, as they leave on their extraordinary excursion, convey with them the expectations, goals, and dreams of a world dazzled by the charm of style.

1.1. Introduction to the Contestants

In the realm of ability rivalries, where dreams are sought after with resolute assurance, candidates are the essence of the show. They are the people who step onto the stage, under the spotlight, to exhibit their interesting skills, from singing and moving to wizardry stunts and gymnastics. Every challenger brings their own story, dreams, and yearnings, causing them the point of convergence of these dazzling shows that to resound with crowds all over the planet.

The prologue to the competitors is a crucial second in any ability contest. It's the main impression the crowd gets of the people who have left on this invigorating excursion. The fervor and apprehensive energy in the air are substantial as the hopefuls stand under the steady gaze of the appointed authorities, the live crowd, and the large numbers watching from their homes. A second represents the intermingling of ability, desire, and opportunity.

Competitors are much of the time driven by an unquenchable enthusiasm for their specialty. They have leveled up their abilities over long stretches of training, confronted various difficulties, and devoted themselves to accomplishing their fantasies. For some, the phase of an ability rivalry addresses the acknowledgment of a long lasting yearning, an opportunity to hit one out of the ballpark, and a venturing stone to their ideal future.

The universe of ability rivalries is assorted and unfathomable. It traverses a wide range of ability and expertise, from singing and moving to parody and assortment acts. Every challenger has a one of a kind ability, and this distinction is commended in the opposition. It is through their exhibitions that contenders convey their particular voices and imagination, offering crowds an enrapturing and various cluster of gifts to respect.

The excursion of competitors is frequently set apart by snapshots of self-revelation and self-awareness. They overcome their feelings of dread, stretch their boundaries, and persistently develop their art. The method involved with planning for an ability contest is a significant endeavor, one that requests steadfast commitment and assurance. Candidates go through thorough preparation, calibrating their abilities and cleaning their demonstrations flawlessly.

While the fervor of performing is a focal part of their excursion, competitors likewise should battle with the tensions and vulnerabilities of contest. The heaviness of assumptions, the expectation of judgment, and the feeling of dread toward dismissal are steady friends. These profound and mental difficulties test their flexibility, pushing them to vanquish their apprehensions and step into the spotlight.

The ability rivalry stage is a stage for candidates to show what them can do. It is where they intend to catch the hearts and minds of both the adjudicators and the crowd. Challengers frequently pick pieces that are profoundly significant to them, mirroring their singular stories, interests, and feelings. It is through these exhibitions that they desire to interface with their crowd on a significant level, rising above the limits of language and culture.

One of the characterizing parts of ability rivalries is the variety of the candidates. They come from various foundations, societies, and age gatherings, exhibiting a wide range of gifts. The stage is a position of inclusivity and opportunity, where ability knows no limits. This variety frequently enhances the opposition, adding profundity and expansiveness to the variety of exhibitions.

Competitors are not simply entertainers; they are additionally narrators. Their demonstrations convey stories that reverberate with crowds, whether through the expressions of a melody, the developments of a dance, or the creativity of a composition. These stories offer a brief look into the lives, dreams, and goals of the contenders, making their exhibitions interesting and motivating.

The excursion of a hopeful isn't restricted to the bounds of a solitary exhibition. In an ability rivalry, they go through numerous rounds, each introducing another test and opportunity to exhibit their flexibility and development. These rounds test their flexibility and their capacity to proceed to enthrall and astonish the adjudicators and the crowd.

In the realm of ability rivalries, candidates likewise experience the extraordinary force of public openness. As their exhibitions air on TV or circulate around the web on the web, contenders become commonly recognized names. They procure fans and devotees who are put resources into their excursions, and their gifts frequently become a well-spring of motivation for other people. The openness acquired through ability rivalries can open ways to new open doors, from proficient agreements to coordinated efforts with laid out craftsmen.

Ability rivalries are many times decided by a board of specialists who assess the contenders' exhibitions. The appointed authorities are liable for giving input and scrutinize as well as for directing the hopefuls on their excursion. Their bits of knowledge and guidance can be priceless to the improvement of the hopefuls' gifts and professions.

Candidates additionally have the amazing chance to gain from their kindred rivals. In the affectionate and frequently serious climate of an ability rivalry, they share encounters, offer help, and manufacture significant associations. These cooperations can be instrumental in their development as entertainers, as they gain bits of knowledge according to alternate points of view and styles.

In the realm of ability rivalries, winning is a sought after dream. The title, the prize, and the acknowledgment are images of approval and achievement. Notwithstanding, it's memorable's vital that the genuine worth of the opposition lies in the actual excursion. For some challengers, the experience of venturing onto the stage and sharing their ability is a triumph by its own doing. It is a demonstration of their mental fortitude, devotion, and the satisfaction of their fantasies.

The universe of ability rivalries reaches out past the stage. Competitors frequently become diplomats of their specialty, moving others to seek after their interests and feature their abilities. Their processes act as a demonstration of the unlimited conceivable outcomes that can be accomplished with devotion and assurance.

All through this book, we will dive into the complex universe of ability rivalries, investigating the accounts of contenders who have actually thought about pursuing their fantasies, beat difficulties, and entranced crowds with their gifts. We will observer the extraordinary force of the stage and the unyielding soul of the people who stand under the watchful eye of the adjudicators and the crowd, planning to transform the universe of diversion.

The excursion of a competitor is an odyssey of self-disclosure, strength, and creative articulation. It is a demonstration of the persevering through charm of ability contests and the general interest with the exceptional capacities that people have. As we adventure into the dazzling accounts of these contenders, we are welcome to commend their mental fortitude, inventiveness, and unrelenting quest for their fantasies.

The universe of ability rivalries keeps on developing, with new ages of contenders prepared to make that big appearance. Their accounts are a demonstration of the getting through force of human innovativeness and the immortal charm of exhibiting one's ability. These contenders are the encapsulation of the visionary's soul, advising us that with enthusiasm and assurance, the sky is the limit. Their processes mirror the general human longing to impart their remarkable gifts to the world, to rouse, and to make a permanent imprint through the groundbreaking force of ability.

1.2. Diverse Backgrounds and Aspirations

In the domain of ability rivalries, the candidates who make that big appearance hail from a kaleidoscope of foundations, each with an extraordinary story to advise and goals to satisfy. These different candidates are the backbone of these contests, addressing a wide cluster of gifts, societies, and encounters that dazzle crowds all over the planet. As we dive into their experiences and desires, we reveal the rich embroidered artwork of human inventiveness and the all inclusive quest for dreams that join challengers, no matter what their beginnings.

Ability rivalries are a mixture of different gifts, incorporating a wide range of abilities and capacities. Whether it's singing, moving, enchantment, parody, or even the most novel and surprising gifts, these rivalries give a phase to people to communicate their innovativeness and dazzle crowds. The variety of gifts in plain view is a demonstration of the vast scope of human capacities and the getting through interest with the exceptional.

What makes ability rivalries really convincing is the hopefuls' accounts. The foundations from which they arise are just about as shifted as their abilities. Competitors frequently come from varying backgrounds, addressing various societies, dialects, and encounters. Some might have been preparing for their second at the center of attention since adolescence, while others find their abilities further down the road.

No matter what their starting point, they share an ongoing idea — the longing to exhibit their capacities and offer their energy with the world.

For some contenders, the excursion starts in their early stages, when they initially find their remarkable gifts. They are driven by an inborn enthusiasm, an unquenchable longing to put themselves out there and offer their gifts with others. The acknowledgment of their gifts frequently comes as a snapshot of enlivening, an acknowledgment that they have an exceptional capacity that separates them.

The way to the stage is frequently set apart by persistence and devotion. Challengers go through long periods of thorough preparation and practice to calibrate their abilities. They train resolutely, frequently under the direction of tutors, mentors, and instructors who assist them with fostering their abilities to their maximum capacity. These tutors assume a significant part in molding the excursion of competitors, giving the direction and backing fundamental for progress.

Notwithstanding their coaches, the help of loved ones is instrumental in the challengers' excursions. The unflinching conviction and consolation from friends and family give the profound food that fills their desire. Families frequently make critical penances to empower hopefuls to seek after their fantasies, from funding illustrations and travel to offering basic encouragement during snapshots of self-question.

The foundations from which candidates arise are just about as different as the gifts they have. A few contenders come from unobtrusive, common foundations, where the quest for a profession in human expression or diversion might be met with wariness or vulnerability. For these people, the ability rivalry stage addresses an opportunity to break liberated from constraints, to follow their interests, and to demonstrate that fantasies can be acknowledged no matter what one's starting points.

Different competitors might come from additional favored foundations, where valuable open doors for preparing and schooling in their picked field are more available. The stage turns into a stage for them to exhibit their capacities and add their voices to the universe of diversion.

Regardless of their benefits, they also face difficulties and tensions to succeed, frequently determined by the heaviness of assumptions.

The foundations of challengers may likewise be set apart by geological variety. Challengers from various districts and nations carry their interesting social impacts to their exhibitions, change up the opposition. The stage turns into where societies meet, and contenders commend their legacy through their gifts, whether it's customary dance, music, or workmanship.

For some candidates, language isn't a hindrance however a resource. Multilingual entertainers can interface with crowds from around the world, getting through etymological limits to convey the general language of music, dance, and workmanship. Their exhibitions reverberate with crowds around the world, featuring the force of ability to rise above borders.

In the realm of ability rivalries, candidates additionally face the test of adjusting their schooling or professions with their quest for their fantasies. Numerous contenders are understudies who shuffle their scholarly obligations with the requesting timetables of practices and exhibitions. For other people, their ability turns into their essential occupation, expecting them to explore the vulnerabilities and monetary difficulties of a lifelong in human expression.

The phases of ability rivalries are eminent for being balancers, where hopefuls from different foundations have a chance to sparkle. No matter what their beginnings, challengers stand on a similar stage under a similar spotlight, where their ability becomes the overwhelming focus. The crowds and judges assess them in view of their abilities, energy, and allure as opposed to their social or financial foundations.

The tryout interaction is in many cases the main significant stage for hopefuls. It is a vital second where they step into the spotlight and present their ability to the appointed authorities and a live crowd. Tryouts are set apart by expectation, energy, and frequently anxiety. The tryouts are where dreams are either understood or broken, where contenders endeavor to make their gifts sparkle in only a couple of moments.

The different foundations of hopefuls likewise bring a great many stories and encounters to the tryouts. A few hopefuls might have confronted individual difficulties, defeating difficulties and impediments that have formed their assurance to succeed. Their exhibitions mirror the flexibility that has brought them through troublesome times.

In the tryouts, challengers likewise express their yearnings and dreams. It is a second where they convey their enthusiasm for their art and their yearning to impart it to a more extensive crowd. Their exhibitions are pervaded with a feeling of direction and a longing to leave an imprint in the realm of diversion. The tryouts offer a stage for them to declare their appearance and spread the word about their gifts for the world.

Contenders from assorted foundations likewise exemplify the all inclusive human quest for dreams and yearnings. They advise us that ability knows no limits and that imagination isn't restricted by topography, economic wellbeing, or social beginnings. Their accounts of assurance and fortitude motivate crowds to pursue their fantasies, no matter what the difficulties they might confront.

The variety of foundations and desires is a demonstration of the force of ability rivalries to open ways to an open door and give a stage to people to accomplish their fantasies. For some challengers, the excursion isn't just about winning the opposition however about influencing the universe of diversion, understanding their energy, and moving others to do likewise.

As we dig into the tales of these different hopefuls, we witness the mind blowing ventures they leave on, the difficulties they survive, and the fantasies they rejuvenate on the stage. Their experiences and goals are an impression of the getting through human soul, the craving to communicate, make, and offer their special gifts with the world.

The universe of ability rivalries stays where variety is praised, where dreams are sought after, and where the widespread language of ability interfaces individuals from varying backgrounds. The challengers who stand on the stage, regardless of their experiences, are symbolic of the human longing to be seen, heard, and celebrated for their inventiveness and ability.

In the parts that follow, we will investigate the dazzling accounts of hopefuls who have thought about pursuing their fantasies and make that big appearance. Their different foundations and desires are a demonstration of the persevering through charm of ability rivalries and the all inclusive interest with the phenomenal capacities that people have. These candidates are the

encapsulation of the visionary's soul, advising us that with enthusiasm and assurance, the sky is the limit. Their processes mirror the all inclusive human longing to impart their novel gifts to the world, to rouse, and to make a permanent imprint through the extraordinary force of ability.

1.3. Casting and Selection Process

In the realm of ability contests, the projecting and choice cycle is the pot where dreams come to fruition and yearnings join. It is the thorough and frequently heart-beating stage where huge number of confident people compete for the sought after an open door to remain on the highlighted stage and grandstand their novel gifts to the world. This interaction is a significant component that revives ability rivalries, molding the story of the challengers' excursions, and eventually, the scene that enthralls crowds around the world.

The projecting and choice cycle is the underlying entryway through which hopeful gifts should pass. It is a multi-layered framework that includes tryouts, callbacks, and extraordinary investigation by a board of judges, projecting chiefs, and makers. The cycle filters through a tremendous pool of ability to recognize the individuals who have the possibility to spellbind crowds and eventually contend on the show.

For challengers, the excursion starts with a fantasy — a fantasy to impart their ability to a more extensive crowd, to accomplish acknowledgment, and to satisfy a long lasting desire. The projecting system is their most memorable chance to change that fantasy into the real world. A second can be loaded up with uneasiness and expectation, as well as the desire for dazzling appointed authorities and getting a put on the show.

The open tryouts are many times the initial step for yearning contenders. These are huge scope occasions held in significant urban communities, where people from different foundations, ages, and gifts assemble to perform under the watchful eye of a board of judges. The open tryouts are known for their long queues and clamoring swarms, as contenders anxiously anticipate their chance to step onto the stage.

The open tryouts are a mixture of gifts, from vocalists and artists to entertainers, performers, and assortment acts. It's an exhibit of the endless scope of human capacities, where people uncover their one of a kind gifts to an insightful board of judges who are entrusted with recognizing the hidden treasures.

The auditionees are driven by their energy, their longing to really establish themselves, and their relentless faith in their abilities. Some have been preparing and leveling up their abilities for quite a long time, while others might be generally new to their art. The tryouts are a balancer, where contenders have the chance to spread the word and stick out, no matter what their experiences.

The tryouts are tied in with displaying specialized abilities as well as about conveying feeling, allure, and stage presence. Contenders should establish a critical connection with the adjudicators and the crowd inside the concise range of their exhibition. The adjudicators are searching for specialized capability as well as for the possibility to enrapture and engage.

One of the extremely important occasions of the projecting system is the hopeful's capacity to transcend apprehension and convey a faultless presentation under tension. The tryouts are frequently extreme, with candidates confronting the adjudicators as well as a live crowd and, sometimes, the strain of time limitations. It is at these times that the genuine capability of competitors is uncovered.

The auditionees frequently go through a blend of feelings — energy, nervousness, and expectation — as they hang tight for their turn. For some, the tryout is a high-stakes second that could be the start of their excursion to distinction. The fantasies and goals that have been held onto for quite a long time rely on these couple of moments of execution.

The adjudicators assume a crucial part in the projecting system. They are a different board of specialists, containing people who have made progress in media outlets, from music and dance to parody and wizardry. Their job is to assess the challengers in view of their ability, stage presence, and potential to dazzle crowds. Their experiences are instrumental in choosing the people who will advance to the following period of the opposition.

The tryouts are frequently a rollercoaster of feelings, with hopefuls getting an extensive variety of criticism from the adjudicators. A few candidates experience celebration as they get thunderous applauses and gleaming commendations, while others face the mistake of dismissal. The projecting system is a situation with two sides, as a stage can drive hopefuls to fame or convey the devastating blow of dismissal.

At times, contenders who are at first dismissed during the open tryouts are allowed a second opportunity through callbacks. Callbacks are a phase of the projecting system where select challengers are welcome to perform again for the adjudicators. This stage fills in as a chance for challengers to show their flexibility and capacity to gain from criticism.

Yet again the callbacks are a close to home rollercoaster of their own, with hopefuls encountering a blend of nervousness and assurance as they get ready to perform. The chance for a callback is a help for the individuals who confronted starting dismissal, an opportunity to vindicate themselves and demonstrate their true capacity.

The callbacks are likewise a demonstration of the groundbreaking force of ability contests. Competitors frequently utilize the criticism from their underlying tryouts to refine their exhibitions, tweak their demonstrations, and carry new components to their introductions.

The interaction fills in as an important growth opportunity, pushing candidates to develop and adjust.

For certain hopefuls, the callbacks address a defining moment. They might have confronted introductory dismissal however have utilized the criticism to drive themselves to a higher level. This versatility and assurance are characteristics that the appointed authorities frequently look for in competitors, as they are demonstrative of the possibility to develop and succeed.

The projecting system isn't simply a grandstand of ability yet additionally a stage for narrating. Challengers frequently share their own accounts, their excursions, and the inspirations driving their goals. These stories give setting and profundity to their exhibitions, permitting the appointed authorities and the crowd to interface with the candidates on a more significant level.

The projecting system is many times formed by the range of abilities that are introduced. The variety of abilities in plain view is a demonstration of the endless scope of human capacities, from old style virtuosos to imaginative and unusual demonstrations. The interaction uncovers the getting through interest with the remarkable and the widespread longing to be enraptured and engaged.

Notwithstanding individual demonstrations, a few contenders likewise structure gatherings or teams to grandstand their gifts. These gathering exhibitions frequently add a component of cooperative energy and variety to the opposition, as contenders team up and complete one another abilities.

All through the projecting system, the adjudicators are entrusted with the difficult occupation of choosing the hopefuls who will progress to the following period of the opposition. Their choices are impacted not just by the specialized capability of the contenders yet in addition by their capability to draw in and engage. The projecting system frequently requires a fragile harmony between assessing the contenders' abilities to ongoing and their true capacity for development.

The variety of gifts, foundations, and goals makes the projecting system a dynamic and complex undertaking. The choices made by the appointed authorities are many times an impression of the scope of gifts and the novel stories that candidates bring to the tryouts. The projecting system isn't just about choosing the best gifts yet in addition about making a different and drawing in setup of competitors.

For those competitors who endure the tryouts and callbacks, the projecting system denotes the start of a groundbreaking excursion. They continue on toward the following period of the opposition, where they will confront more difficulties, develop as entertainers, and have the valuable chance to spellbind and engage a worldwide crowd.

The projecting system is a demonstration of the charm of ability rivalries, where dreams are sought after, and yearnings are understood. It is a passage through which people from different foundations have the open door to feature their remarkable gifts, interface with crowds, and pursue their fantasies. The projecting system is a festival of inventiveness, variety, and the all inclusive interest with the phenomenal capacities that people have.

In the parts that follow, we will investigate the enrapturing excursions of the competitors who have gone through the cauldron of the projecting and choice cycle. Their accounts mirror the groundbreaking force of ability contests and the widespread human longing to pursue dreams, enrapture crowds, and make history. The projecting system isn't just about choosing the best gifts yet in addition about making a different and drawing in setup of candidates who will motivate, engage, and stun.

Chapter Two

The Fashion World Unveiled

The universe of style is a hypnotizing domain that persistently dazzles, rehashes, and pushes the limits of imagination and self-articulation. Past the gleaming runway shows and reflexive magazine covers lies a dynamic and diverse industry that contacts each edge of the globe, impacting society, workmanship, and business. Style is something other than dress; it is a strong medium through which people and planners convey their remarkable dreams, thoughts, and feelings. In this investigation of the design world, we will dive into the unpredictable embroidery of this industry, from its set of experiences and social importance to the advancing elements of the cutting edge style scene.

The historical backdrop of design is a distinctive embroidery woven with strings of workmanship, culture, and cultural change. Design, as we grasp it today, has advanced over hundreds of years, with every period bringing its unmistakable styles, patterns, and impacts. It is a living demonstration of the consistently moving elements of human articulation and the unending longing for change and rehash.

The starting points of style can be followed back to the beginning of human advancement, while apparel was fundamentally useful, intended to give insurance and solace. Be that as it may, even in these early times, people showed a longing to enhance themselves, utilizing normal materials like quills, shells, and creature stows away to make enriching dress and embellishments.

As social orders developed, fashion did as well. Old civilizations like Egypt, Greece, and Rome fostered their own particular styles, frequently affected by their social convictions, environment, and accessible materials. In these social orders, clothing turned into an image of status, riches, and even religion. The curtain of frocks in Rome or the complicated beadwork of antiquated African clans both mirrored the qualities and customs of their separate societies.

The Medieval times saw the rise of exceptionally adapted and frequently luxurious apparel, particularly among the respectability. Intricate, resplendent articles of clothing, like the unsettled collars and unpredictable weaving of the Renaissance, were made with accuracy and craftsmanship, meaning the power and societal position of the people who wore them.

The Modern Unrest of the eighteenth and nineteenth hundreds of years achieved tremendous changes in style. Large scale manufacturing, the accessibility of new textures, and the development of the material business democratized design partially. Clothing was presently not the selective space of the affluent tip top; it turned out to be more available to the more extensive populace.

In the twentieth 100 years, style went through a progression of emotional shifts, to a great extent impacted by cultural changes and worldwide occasions. The 1920s, for example, were set apart by the "Thundering Twenties," a period portrayed by short hemlines, strong prints, and the rise of the "flapper" style that represented ladies' newly discovered opportunity and freedom. This period additionally saw the ascent of famous style creators like Coco Chanel, who altered ladies' style with her basic, exquisite plans.

The 1960s introduced a social unrest that resounded through style. The young development and nonconformity assumed a huge part in reshaping style, with originators like Mary Quant presenting miniskirts and striking, creative styles that split away from the moderate standards of earlier many years. The 1960s were a time of trial and error, self-articulation, and a push against the laid out request, all of which got comfortable with themselves through design.

The 1980s considered an emotional change in style to be well, with an emphasis on overabundance, strong varieties, and power dressing. The period of shoulder braces, neon, and strong prints exemplified the extravagance and self-assuredness of the time. Interestingly, the 1990s embraced moderation, with planners like Calvin Klein and Helmut Lang driving the way.

The effortlessness of the "grit" style, promoted by groups like Nirvana, altogether affected style during this period.

In the 21st 100 years, design keeps on developing quickly, impacted by mechanical progressions, globalization, and the changing elements of the computerized age. Quick style, portrayed by its capacity to rapidly create and convey minimal expense, in vogue clothing, has turned into a predominant power in the business, reshaping buyer assumptions and the creation cycle.

Also, design is progressively meeting with innovation. Wearable innovation, 3D printing, and inventive materials are pushing the limits of what dress can do and how it can incorporate with our regular routines. The combination of design and innovation is making new roads for self-articulation and the investigation of style.

The design business isn't just about clothing; it is additionally a persuasive piece of culture and character. Design has been a vehicle for self-articulation, an impression of social change, and an image of resistance and similarity. It is a medium through which people and creators can pass on their exceptional points of view, values, and messages. Whether it's involving clothing as a type of dissent or as a festival of social legacy, design assumes an essential part in forming cultural standards and pushing limits.

In the domain of high fashion, where originators make exceptional, carefully created pieces, style is raised to a fine art. These creators are frequently worshipped for their capacity to mix imagination, craftsmanship, and development. High fashion embodies the most significant level of style, where pieces of clothing are hand tailored with the greatest amount of accuracy, including extravagant textures, complex embellishments, and cutting edge plans.

Style likewise fills in for the purpose of social articulation and character. It is a way for people to interface with their legacy, convey their convictions, and commend their foundations. Customary attire, like the kimono in Japan, the sari in India, or the kente material in Africa, mirrors the rich woven artwork of social variety and customs that style exemplifies.

Design is a vehicle for social change and a stage for activism. Since forever ago, clothing has been utilized to provoke standards and point out friendly and policy centered issues. From the suffragettes wearing white during the battle for ladies' privileges to the LGBTQ+ people group's utilization of the rainbow banner on the side of fairness, design has been an integral asset for bringing issues to light and advancing change.

Lately, the design business has shown a rising obligation to manageability and moral practices. The natural effect of quick design and the moral worries encompassing work rehearses have incited a reexamination of the business' norms. Numerous creators and brands are currently zeroing in on eco-accommodating materials, mindful obtaining, and fair work works on, flagging a shift towards a more maintainable and socially cognizant design scene.

The design world is a tremendous biological system that incorporates a bunch of jobs, from creators and models to photographic artists, beauticians, and advertisers. These people add to the creation, show, and spread of design, each assuming a critical part in molding the business. Behind the marvelousness and style of runway shows and design magazines lies a complicated organization of experts who make it all conceivable.

Style planners are the modelers of the business, the inventive visionaries who consider and rejuvenate clothing. They are liable for planning assortments that mirror their one of a kind tasteful, motivations, and messages. A fashioner's work includes making draws, choosing textures, and managing the whole presentation cycle to change their vision into the real world.

Models are the living materials whereupon creators paint their manifestations. They are answerable for carrying life and development to the dress, diverting it from a static piece into a dynamic, enthralling vision. Models are picked in light of their physical make-up, presence, and capacity to convey the fashioner's vision on the runway or in photoshoots.

Photographic artists assume an essential part in catching and introducing design to the world. They are answerable for making an interpretation of the creator's vision into spellbinding pictures. Style photography is an artistic expression in itself, known for its imagination, piece, and capacity to summon feeling and want.

Beauticians are the entertainers in the background, organizing and planning the outfits and embellishments that models wear during photoshoots and runway shows. They have an intrinsic fashion instinct and a sharp eye for detail, it is perfectly assembled to guarantee that each look.

Cosmetics specialists and hairdressers are liable for improving the general look of models, finishing the change into the ideal picture. Their creativity frequently assumes a urgent part in conveying the temperament and subject of an assortment, whether it's through strong, vanguard looks or normal, downplayed magnificence.

The style business is additionally vigorously dependent on showcasing and marking. Marketing specialists, advertisers, and publicists are liable for making whiz around assortments and brands. Their work includes building a picture, advancing style shows, and drawing in with general society through different media channels.

Design news-casting and style pundits are essential to the business' discourse. They give experiences, audits, and investigation of assortments, architects, and patterns. Their work shapes the account of design, assisting with characterizing what is stylish and what isn't.

The universe of design isn't without its difficulties and discussions. The business has confronted analysis for advancing unreasonable magnificence principles, adding to natural issues through over the top waste and contamination, and for moral worries with respect to work rehearses in certain areas. These issues have incited a reconsideration of the style world's practices and the development of developments upholding for change.

2.1. The Glitz and Glamour of the Fashion Industry

The style business, with its amazing runway shows, extravagant creator assortments, and big name studded occasions, is inseparable from glamour and charm. An industry flourishes with the charm of extravagance, style, and inventive articulation, dazzling crowds all over the planet with its capacity to move us into a universe of excellence and excess. The style business isn't just about clothing; it is a phase where dreams, masterfulness, and yearnings merge, making a display that reverberates with the human craving for magnificence and self-articulation.

The core of the style business beats on the runways of the world's design capitals, from Paris and Milan to New York and London. Style weeks, which happen semi-yearly in these notorious urban communities, are the central marks of the business, exhibiting the most recent assortments from prestigious planners. These occasions are significantly more than simply a showcase of dress; they are excellent, dramatic creations that offer a brief look into the imaginativeness, craftsmanship, and narrating that characterize the design world.

Style weeks are a tornado of action, drawing creators, models, superstars, and design lovers from all sides of the globe. The runways are embellished with intricate sets, music, and lighting that upgrade the experience. Every assortment is a painstakingly arranged exhibition, with models swaggering down the catwalk to disclose the creator's manifestations. The energy and fervor in the air are substantial, as the crowd enthusiastically expects the following sensational gathering.

Originators are the maestros of this style orchestra. They consider and make assortments that act as their imaginative articulations, communicating their one of a kind vision, motivation, and story. The planner's job isn't restricted to portraying articles of clothing; it additionally includes choosing textures, exploring different avenues regarding surfaces, and supervising the craftsmanship of each piece. These assortments frequently act as an impression of the originator's innovative development, an indication of their imaginative excursion and motivations.

The style and fabulousness of the runway shows stretch out to the first line, where superstars, design editors, purchasers, and forces to be reckoned with assemble to observe the scene. It is where the design world blends with the universe of diversion and media, making a cooperative energy of inventive powers. Superstars wearing the most recent architect pieces are in many cases at the center of attention, becoming design symbols by their own doing and molding patterns with their style decisions.

The runway isn't simply a stage for planners to feature their assortments; it is likewise a road for models to leave an imprint. Models are the living materials whereupon architects' manifestations show some signs of life. Their presence on the runway is spellbinding, as they revive clothing, implanting it with development and beauty. Models exemplify the quintessence of the assortment, passing the creator's vision on through their walk, articulation, and mentality.

Demonstrating is an exceptionally cutthroat field, with models competing for desired spots in runway shows and missions. The design business has advanced to embrace variety, and models come in different sizes, ages, and nationalities, mirroring the push for inclusivity and portrayal. The runway is at this point not selective to tall, super thin models; it is a space where different magnificence norms and body types are praised.

The existence of a model is requesting, including thorough physical and mental planning. Models should keep up with their physical make-up, persevere through extended periods of time of fittings and practices, and stay tough notwithstanding analysis. They likewise as often as possible travel the globe, taking part in runway shows and photoshoots, which can be both thrilling and debilitating.

In the background, the outcome of a runway show is organized by a group of experts who work enthusiastically to carry the creator's vision to completion. Cosmetics craftsmen and beauticians make looks that supplement the dress and convey the ideal state of mind of the assortment. The decision of music, lighting, and set plan adds layers of climate and narrating to the show.

Design weeks are likewise critical for the style business concerning business and trade. Purchasers, style writers, and editors go to these occasions to review assortments and make choices for their retail locations or distributions. The plans that establish areas of strength for a with the runway frequently become the style that impact buyer decisions in the seasons to come.

Notwithstanding the runway shows, style weeks are joined by a tornado of gatherings, occasions, and all-nighters, went to by famous people, originators, and industry insiders. These get-togethers are a chance for systems administration, building connections, and commending the finish of long stretches of difficult work. Design weeks are an embodiment of the fabulous side of the business, where innovativeness merges with trade.

While the runway shows and style weeks are a zenith of the design business, the universe of high style stretches out past the fabulousness and excitement of the catwalk. At its center, high style is described by its selectiveness, craftsmanship, and the epitome of masterfulness. High fashion, specifically, is the embodiment of extravagance and refinement, where articles of clothing are carefully assembled with accuracy and scrupulousness.

High fashion is the apex of design, addressing the creativity and craftsmanship of the business. It is portrayed by its selectiveness, with pieces of clothing made as unique pieces or in extremely restricted amounts. The fastidious meticulousness, the utilization of lavish materials, and the exact handwork in making each piece of clothing make high fashion a demonstration of the greatest degree of craftsmanship.

Architects who adventure into the domain of high fashion are frequently venerated for their imaginative ability. Their assortments are a combination of style and workmanship, highlighting vanguard plans, perplexing embellishments, and flighty materials. High fashion assortments are much of the time a stage for planners to push the limits of inventiveness, unconstrained by the common sense and large scale manufacturing requests of prepared to-wear style.

The most common way of making high fashion is work escalated, with exceptionally talented craftsmans and specialists working constantly to rejuvenate the planner's vision. From the determination of textures to the fastidious weaving and hand-sewn gets done, each article of clothing is an encapsulation of accuracy and commitment. The outcome is a masterpiece that rises above style, praised for its resourcefulness and imaginative articulation.

The charm of high fashion stretches out to a select customers, including eminence, big names, and knowing people who value the craftsmanship and independence of these manifestations. High fashion clients look for articles of clothing that fit impeccably as well as mirror their particular style and inclinations. The eliteness of high fashion guarantees that clients are gaining a piece of style history and imaginativeness.

The style business' fabulousness isn't restricted to the high fashion ateliers and runway shows; it additionally envelops the universe of design article and photography. Design photography, specifically, is a work of art in itself, known for its imagination, sythesis, and capacity to summon feeling and want. It assumes a critical part in conveying the temperament, story, and stylish of assortments.

Style picture takers are the visionaries behind the focal point, liable for making an interpretation of the architect's manifestations into charming pictures. They work intimately with models, beauticians, cosmetics craftsmen, and inventive chiefs to create striking visuals that convey the substance of the style. Their work is many times described by its advancement, excellence, and narrating.

The pages of design magazines are a material for style photography. Article spreads highlight models enhanced in creator clothing, set against imaginative sceneries and areas that add to the general story. Style photography is a powerful medium that helps shape patterns, rouse buyers, and convey the creative quintessence of assortments.

The design business is additionally formed by beauticians, who curate and direction the outfits, embellishments, and looks highlighted in photoshoots and article spreads. Beauticians have an inborn instinct with regards to fashion and a sharp eye for detail, it is faultlessly assembled to guarantee that each look. They assume a vital part in conveying the vision of originators and photographic artists and making outwardly convincing stories.

Style columnists and design pundits are instrumental in molding the business' exchange. They give experiences, surveys, and examination of assortments, fashioners, and patterns, assisting with characterizing what is stylish and what isn't. The style media impacts shopper decisions and discernments, featuring the meaning of an assortment's gathering in the press.

The fabulousness and style of the design business reach out past the pages of magazines and the runways; it is additionally reflected in the red floor coverings and stupendous occasions that charm the public's creative mind. Grant functions, film celebrations, and debuts are events for big names to grandstand the most recent originator manifestations, making design an essential piece of the amusement world.

The association among design and amusement is advantageous. Superstars, frequently alluded to as "style symbols," assume a huge part in forming style and advancing brands. Their presence on honorary pathway and at public occasions creates worldwide consideration, making them persuasive figures in the design world.

Creators and design houses perceive the impact of VIPs and frequently team up with them, making custom pieces or manufacturing brand associations. These joint efforts span the universes of amusement and design, further improving the marvelousness and perceivability of the two businesses.

2.2. Behind-the-Scenes of a Model's Life

The universe of style and demonstrating, with its captivating outside, is many times seen from a perspective of charm and polish. It invokes pictures of strikingly lovely people, stepping certainly down runways, gracing the fronts of high-style magazines, and blending with superstars. Notwithstanding, underneath this exterior lies a complicated, requesting, and exceptionally serious industry, where models explore a many-sided snare of provokes and potential chances to do something worth remembering. In this investigation of the in the background life of a model, we dive into the universe of castings, appointments, the requests of physical and mental upkeep, the force of portrayal, and the groundbreaking effect of innovation.

The excursion of a model frequently starts with a projecting. Castings are the soul of the style business, the beginning stage where models, no matter what their degree of involvement or acknowledgment, come to compete for chances to walk the runways, highlight in photoshoots, or star in publicizing efforts. These tryout like occasions are tied in with exhibiting looks and characters as well as about lining up with the vision of planners, brands, and projecting chiefs.

Models normally go to various castings every day, introducing themselves to a board of industry experts who assess their expected reasonableness for impending tasks. The opposition is savage, with scores of models wanting to get a sought after spot. At castings, reliability and incredible skill are fundamental, as a solitary botched open door can mean the contrast among progress and lack of clarity.

Actual properties assume a basic part in projecting determination. Models are regularly sorted by level, estimations, and explicit actual highlights to fit the necessities of a specific venture or brand. While the design business has gained ground in embracing different body types and appearances, there stays a level of strain to adjust to customary norms of excellence.

The projecting system isn't just about actual traits yet additionally about conveying character and presence. Models should ooze certainty, charm, and the capacity to line up with the brand's ethos and the architect's vision. The manner in which they walk, posture, and convey themselves frequently assumes an essential part in their determination.

For yearning models, the projecting system is a considerable excursion that requests flexibility and versatility. Dismissals are normal, and models figure out how to foster a toughness. Numerous castings end with respectful expressions of gratitude yet no appointments, passing on models to consider how they can improve for the following an open door.

Callbacks are the second period of the projecting system, where a select gathering of models are welcome to meet with the client, creator, or projecting chief. Callbacks address a positive development, as they demonstrate a level of interest from the client. During callbacks, models might take a stab at outfits, posture for photographs, and participate in discussions to decide if they are an ideal choice for the undertaking.

The requesting idea of castings and callbacks makes it fundamental for models to deal with their physical and mental prosperity. Keeping a sound way of life, standard activity, and a reasonable eating routine are about appearance as well as about endurance and perseverance. Models should have the actual solidarity to get through extended periods, frequently in awkward circumstances, for example, strolling in transcending heels or confronting openness to brilliant lights during photoshoots.

The strain to keep a particular body shape and size is a point that has ignited a lot of discussion in the style business. While progress has been made in embracing variety and body energy, the assumptions put on models to keep a specific constitution are as yet a reality. Many models feel the kind of these assumptions, prompting worries about self-perception, confidence, and psychological well-being.

The psychological flexibility of models is tried in a calling that frequently accompanies dismissal and analysis. The demonstrating scene can be unforgiving, with models confronting strain to adjust to industry guidelines of magnificence, stroll with certainty, and keep up with impressive skill even notwithstanding dismissal. Models frequently need to foster areas of strength for an of self and profound flexibility to explore these difficulties.

Notwithstanding the tensions of projecting and actual upkeep, models likewise wrestle with the capriciousness of their timetables. The displaying scene works on a tight timetable, with last-minute changes, travel, and long working hours. The capacity to adjust to these unique requests is critical for progress.

Travel is a crucial part of a model's life. Models frequently end up venturing to various urban communities, nations, and even mainlands to satisfy their tasks. These regular movements might appear to be energizing yet can be both genuinely and sincerely burdening. Overseeing time regions, acclimating to new societies, and adapting to achiness to go home are an integral part of the movement experience for models.

One more part of the model's life is the complex job they play. Past the runway, models might take part in different sorts of demonstrating, including business, publication, and publicizing work. These jobs might require various abilities, from oozing character and energy in business shoots to pausing dramatically in publication work. The flexibility and adaptability of models are resources that assist them with flourishing in a profoundly cutthroat climate.

The force of portrayal is one more basic part of the demonstrating scene. Throughout the long term, there has been a developing push for variety and inclusivity in the business. Models of various ethnic foundations, body types, and orientation characters are presently progressively apparent on runways and in crusades. This change in portrayal mirrors the business' developing acknowledgment of the significance of inclusivity and the need to mirror the assorted world we live in.

The effect of portrayal goes past the style world. A wellspring of motivation for people have long felt underestimated or underrepresented in media and promoting. Seeing models who appear as though them helps support confidence and enables people to embrace their exceptional excellence and personalities.

Innovation plays had a groundbreaking impact in the demonstrating business. The ascent of web-based entertainment and computerized stages has given models an immediate line to crowds and clients. Models can now feature their portfolios, characters, and in the background minutes through Instagram, TikTok, YouTube, and different stages. These computerized channels have furnished models with the potential chance to fabricate their image, interface with fans, and even adapt their impact.

Web-based entertainment powerhouses are a rising power in the demonstrating scene. Models with major areas of strength for a presence and a critical following can use their computerized impact to get rewarding organizations and brand joint efforts. This shift has extended the meaning of displaying and made new roads for progress.

Innovation has additionally influenced how models are explored. Conventional exploring in the design world included headhunters and scouts going to occasions, castings, and, surprisingly, scanning the roads for likely models. In the computerized age, exploring has extended to virtual entertainment, where scouts and offices find new ability through Instagram and different stages. The democratization of exploring has set out open doors for hopeful models to be seen without fundamentally sticking to conventional projecting cycles.

The elements of the style and demonstrating industry are consistently developing, molded by shifts in social standards, mechanical advances, and the aggregate endeavors to embrace variety and inclusivity. The existence of a model is one of transformation, flexibility, and steadiness, where the excursion to progress is set apart by dismissal, analysis, and the quest for self-strengthening.

As we investigate the in the background life of a model, we gain knowledge into the complex world that reaches out past the runway and the impressive photoshoots. It is an existence where models explore the erratic, requesting nature of the business, keep up with physical and mental prosperity, and influence the force of portrayal and innovation to do something worth remembering. The displaying scene is an impression of the business' development, as it keeps on rethinking magnificence, challenge standards, and praise the variety and uniqueness of people from varying backgrounds.

2.3. The Role of Mentors and Industry Experts

Inside the style and demonstrating industry, achievement not entirely set in stone by looks, ability, or open doors; direction and mentorship assume a significant part in the development and improvement of models. The impact of coaches and industry specialists couldn't possibly be more significant. They act as reference points of shrewdness, experience, and backing, assisting models with exploring the intricacies of the calling, pursue informed decisions, and saddle their true capacity. In this investigation of the job of tutors and industry specialists, we dive into the manners by which old pros enable arising abilities, share their significant experiences, and add to the change of the business.

Mentorship in the style and displaying industry is a dynamic and fundamental connection between a tutor, an accomplished and proficient figure, and a mentee, a less experienced individual looking for direction and backing. It is an organization established on the trading of information, counsel, and support, encouraging the mentee's private and expert development.

Guides can be people with assorted jobs inside the business, from fruitful models and style fashioners to projecting chiefs, photographic artists, specialists, and beauticians. What joins them is their amassed information and experience, which they liberally offer to assist with forming the professions and lives of arising models. Coaching connections frequently emerge naturally, started by the tutor or looked for by the mentee.

Coaches offer important direction to models, especially the individuals who are at the start of their professions. They assist arising abilities with exploring the complexities of the business, from understanding the business parts of demonstrating to furnishing bits of knowledge into overseeing associations with clients and organizations. Coaches additionally help models in making their own image and picture, offering guidance on style, show, and portfolio advancement.

One of the essential jobs of coaches is to assist models with leveling up their abilities and refine their art. They give valuable input on presenting, runway strolls, and articulations. This mentorship goes past specialized exhortation; it includes sustaining fearlessness and self-conviction, urgent characteristics for progress in the demonstrating scene.

Guides additionally offer help and support, particularly notwithstanding difficulties, dismissals, and the strain to satisfy industry guidelines. They assist models with building versatility, foster capacity to understand individuals on a deeper level, and figure out how to adjust to the consistently changing requests of the calling. This everyday encouragement is crucial in an industry where dismissal is normal and can negatively affect confidence.

Additionally, coaches can help models in arriving at informed conclusions about the open doors and offers they get. They assist models with knowing which ventures line up with their drawn out objectives and values, guaranteeing that they stay away from traps and expected abuse. The direction tutors give reaches out to issues of agreements, exchanges, and moral contemplations.

For arising models, mentorship offers a help to a world that can frequently appear to be overwhelming and new. A wellspring of shrewdness and knowledge helps models get by as well as flourish in the profoundly cutthroat and consistently developing industry. Mentorship adds to the expert and self-improvement of models, permitting them to settle on better decisions, construct enduring connections, and arrive at their maximum capacity.

The style and demonstrating industry isn't static; it is constantly formed by the aggregate endeavors of experts who impact its direction. Industry specialists, including prepared fashioners, photographic artists, specialists, and other key figures, are instrumental in starting precedents, driving advancements, and forming the general scene of the business. Their job reaches out past their singular accomplishments; it incorporates their commitment to the bigger business biological system.

Originators, for example, are at the front line of the style business, answerable for considering and making assortments that enamor crowds and set the vibe for future patterns. Architects are trailblazers, with their assortments impacting what buyers wear and how they see style. Their plans frequently rise above the domain of apparel, molding society and self-articulation.

Photographic artists assume a significant part in catching and introducing style to the world. They are the narrators who make an interpretation of an originator's vision into spellbinding pictures. Design photography is a work of art known for its imagination, arrangement, and capacity to bring out feeling and want. Photographic artists have the ability to make design famous, transforming pieces of clothing into masterpieces.

Demonstrating offices and specialists are fundamental for the business' working, filling in as middle people among models and clients. Specialists assume a critical part in exploring and addressing models, getting appointments, and arranging contracts. They are specialists in distinguishing ability, sustaining professions, and exploring the serious scene of the business.

Beauticians are the entertainers in the background, organizing and planning the outfits and frill that models wear during photoshoots and runway shows. They have an inborn fashion instinct and a sharp eye for detail, it is faultlessly assembled to guarantee that each look.

Beauticians assume a vital part in conveying the vision of fashioners and picture takers.

Hair and cosmetics craftsmen are liable for improving the general look of models, finishing their change into the ideal picture. Their masterfulness frequently assumes a vital part in conveying the mind-set and topic of an assortment, whether it's through strong, cutting edge looks or regular, downplayed excellence.

Mentorship and direction presented by industry specialists stretch out past individual models to impact the bigger business scene. Originators, photographic artists, specialists, and different experts assume a part in forming the stories and upsides of the business. Their decisions in projecting, imaginative heading, and narrating add to how design is seen, making way for patterns and affecting cultural standards.

Moreover, industry specialists have the ability to advance moral and supportable practices inside the style world. Fashioners who champion dependable obtaining, eco-accommodating materials, and moral creation processes add to a more maintainable industry. Moreover, picture takers, beauticians, and specialists who support variety and inclusivity can impact the business to embrace portrayal and challenge obsolete excellence standards.

The universe of high style and high fashion, with its obligation to craftsmanship and masterfulness, is driven by originators who represent imagination and advancement. High fashion assortments are famous for their unique pieces, carefully created and celebrated for their richness and refinement. The plans of high fashion planners frequently rise above apparel, pushing the limits of imagination and rethinking the connection among style and craftsmanship.

The effect of industry specialists stretches out to the change of the demonstrating business itself. As of late, there has been a developing push for variety and inclusivity in the demonstrating scene, to a great extent driven by industry specialists who advocate for portrayal of people of all races, body types, and foundations. This shift has impacted the business, provoking changes in projecting practices, runway shows, and publicizing efforts.

Inclusivity and variety in the design and displaying industry are an impression of changing cultural standards as well as an acknowledgment of the business' part in impacting view of excellence and self-esteem. Industry specialists who champion these qualities add to a more comprehensive and delegate industry, cultivating a feeling of strengthening and self-acknowledgment among people.

Supportability is another field where industry specialists are having an effect. The design business' ecological effect, including issues of waste and contamination, has incited a reexamination of practices. Creators, offices, and different experts who underwrite economical materials, moral work rehearses, and capable obtaining are assisting with moving the business toward additional naturally cognizant decisions.

Style weeks, with their persuasive runway shows, are likewise stages where industry specialists make some meaningful difference. These occasions uncover the most recent assortments as well as give a space to planners, models, and different experts to grandstand their imaginative dreams and developments. The patterns and styles introduced during design weeks frequently set the vibe for the seasons to come.

The force of industry specialists stretches out past the regular style cycle. In the period of advanced media and innovation, fashioners, picture takers, and different experts have tackled the capability of online stages to contact worldwide crowds. Virtual entertainment, design web journals, and internet business have become persuasive roads for industry specialists to associate with purchasers, advance their work, and even reclassify the idea of the business.

The connection between guides, industry specialists, and arising gifts is a harmonious one, with each gathering adding to the next's development and achievement. Mentorship offers models an important emotionally supportive network and the insight to explore the intricacies of the calling. Simultaneously, arising gifts mix the business with new viewpoints, energy, and advancement, assisting with pushing the limits of what is conceivable.

As models progress in their professions, they frequently change into the job of industry specialists and guides themselves. Their encounters and experiences, acquired through long stretches of demonstrating, position them to direct and move the up and coming age of models. This propagation of information and backing is fundamental for the business' ceaseless development and advancement.

3

Chapter Three

The Challenges

The design and demonstrating industry, with its charm and style, is a domain of dreams and yearnings. Nonetheless, it is likewise a world laden with difficulties, intricacies, and requesting assumptions. For models and experts inside the business, the way to progress is frequently set apart by impediments that require flexibility, versatility, and tirelessness. In this investigation of the difficulties looked by models and those engaged with the business, we dive into issues going from self-perception tensions to emotional well-being, the cutthroat scene, moral worries, and the consistently advancing requests of the calling.

Quite possibly of the most noticeable and well established challenge in the demonstrating business is the strain to adjust to explicit excellence norms, especially with respect to body shape and size. Models are supposed to meet particular estimations, with an accentuation on tall and thin figures. While the business has taken critical steps in embracing variety and body energy as of late, there stays a level of strain to adjust to conventional beliefs of magnificence.

This tension can significantly affect the confidence and self-perception of models, as they endeavor to meet industry assumptions.

The quest for a particular body shape might prompt undesirable practices, like outrageous counting calories or over-working out, to keep up with their appearance. These practices can negatively affect physical and psychological well-being, adding to issues like dietary problems, tension, and wretchedness.

The displaying scene's assumptions reach out to other actual characteristics, including facial elements, complexion, and hair surface. Models frequently experience segregation in light of these variables, prompting inconsistent open doors and portrayal. As the business keeps on embracing variety and inclusivity, models of various foundations and appearances are testing these obsolete standards.

Emotional well-being is a huge worry in the displaying business, as models face one of a kind stressors that can influence their mental prosperity. The strain to keep a particular appearance, manage consistent dismissal, and adapt to the requesting idea of the calling can add to pressure, nervousness, and wretchedness. The displaying scene's accentuation on picture and flawlessness can worsen emotional wellness challenges.

The transient and flighty nature of the displaying calling can likewise be a wellspring of uneasiness for models. The vulnerability of appointments, the consistent need to adjust to new conditions and timetables, and the potential for significant stretches without work can make monetary and close to home flimsiness. Models frequently experience the nervousness of not knowing when their next task will come.

The cutthroat scene of the demonstrating business is another huge test. The calling is exceptionally cutthroat, with a huge pool of models competing for restricted open doors. The projecting and tryout process is requesting, with various models going to tries out for a solitary spot in a runway show or mission. The strain to stick out and get appointments can be extreme, prompting pressure and self-question.

In addition, the transient and questionable nature of the displaying calling can prompt monetary shakiness. Many models experience periods without work, and the pay from displaying can be conflicting.

Subsequently, models frequently need to foster monetary versatility and plan for periods when they might not have appointments.

The strain to keep a particular appearance and body shape can likewise add to monetary expenses, as models might put resources into fitness coaches, unique eating regimens, and magnificence medicines. The quest for flawlessness and the craving to satisfy industry guidelines can monetarily charge.

Moral worries are common in the design and displaying industry, with progressing conversations about issues, for example, work practices, variety, and maintainability. Work rehearses in certain districts have raised moral worries, including issues connected with fair compensation, working circumstances, and youngster work. Models have a stake in pushing for moral practices and working circumstances in the business.

Variety and portrayal have been focal subjects of conversation as of late, with requires the business to turn out to be more comprehensive. Models from different racial foundations, body types, and orientation personalities have looked for more prominent portrayal and open doors. The push for variety and inclusivity has prompted positive changes, with numerous creators and brands embracing a more extensive scope of models in their missions and runway shows.

Supportability is one more moral worry in the style business. Quick design, described by its superfluity and the utilization of non-biodegradable materials, has raised worries about the business' commitment to contamination and waste. Many models, alongside industry experts, are upholding for additional supportable practices, from utilizing eco-accommodating textures to advancing reusing and capable obtaining.

Models are likewise much of the time exposed to moral difficulties with respect to the tasks they decide to take part in. They might confront choices about working with brands that don't line up with their qualities, whether because of moral or political reasons. These choices can be intricate, as models gauge their profession amazing open doors against their own convictions.

The requests of the demonstrating calling can influence individual connections and public activity. The capricious timetable, successive travel, and long working hours can make it trying to keep a steady balance between fun and serious activities. Models might need to make penances concerning family and individual responsibilities, missing significant occasions and social affairs.

Moreover, the demonstrating business is known for its relationship with gatherings, occasions, and get-togethers. Models frequently end up in conditions where liquor and substance use are common. These circumstances can challenge, as models explore peer strain and pursue decisions that line up with their qualities and prosperity.

Models, particularly while beginning their professions, may experience corrupt people or substances that exploit their freshness. Tricks and manipulative practices exist in the business, from false offices to picture takers looking to take advantage of models. Figuring out how to recognize and safeguard themselves from such practices is a significant part of a model's schooling.

The demonstrating scene's accentuation on picture and flawlessness can add to the improvement of a presentation character, where models might battle to isolate their on-camera persona from their actual selves. This can bring about a feeling of detachment from their genuine character and feelings. Fostering areas of strength for an of self and mindfulness is fundamental to explore these difficulties.

The worldwide idea of the demonstrating business frequently expects models to travel broadly and work in different nations and societies. While this can be an enhancing experience, it can likewise introduce difficulties connected with social contrasts, language obstructions, and transformation to new conditions. Models should adjust rapidly to various social standards, customs, and working circumstances.

Exploring connections inside the business can challenge, as models work intimately with photographic artists, beauticians, cosmetics craftsmen, and different experts. Models frequently need to lay out limits and guarantee their solace and wellbeing on set. The dynamic among models and industry experts requires common regard and impressive skill.

In the advanced age, models likewise face the test of dealing with their web-based presence and virtual entertainment profiles. The strain to introduce a cleaned and organized picture via virtual entertainment can sincerely burden, as models explore the assumptions for keeping a specific public picture while keeping up with their credibility.

In addition, models need to safeguard their computerized security, as the web-based world can be a space for savages, cyberbullying, and obtrusive individual requests. Overseeing online entertainment and the public view of one's very own life can be a requesting part of a model's profession.

The demonstrating business is a steadily developing scene that answers cultural movements, social changes, and mechanical advances. As innovation reshapes the business, models are confronted with new difficulties connected with advanced demonstrating and online substance creation. The ascent of virtual entertainment powerhouses and the obscuring of lines between customary demonstrating and force to be reckoned with professions have added intricacy to the business.

The difficulties looked by models and industry experts highlight the requirement for help, assets, and drives that advance prosperity and moral practices. Associations and backing bunches inside the business are attempting to address these difficulties, from elevating emotional well-being attention to pushing for different portrayal and economical practices.

The demonstrating calling is a dynamic and multi-layered world that requests versatility, flexibility, and a pledge to taking care of oneself. A way expects models to explore the strain to adjust to explicit excellence principles, deal with their psychological well-being, flourish in a serious scene, address moral worries, and adjust to the developing requests of the business.

Even with these difficulties, models frequently track down strength in the help of guides, industry specialists, and support bunches that champion moral practices, variety, and inclusivity. They figure out how to embrace their one of a kind personalities, state their qualities, and tackle the force of portrayal to shape the business' future. The difficulties of the displaying scene are impediments as well as any open doors for development, change, and positive change.

3.1. Overview of the Competition Format

In the unique universe of design and displaying, the excursion from hopeful ability to prestigious model frequently includes taking part in different rivalries and challenges. These occasions act as stages for arising models to exhibit their abilities, gain openness, and launch their professions. In this exhaustive outline of the opposition design, we dive into the construction, importance, and effect of displaying challenges, offering understanding into the valuable open doors they give and the difficulties they present.

Demonstrating contests have been instrumental in molding the professions of numerous famous models. These challenges are intended to recognize, support, and lift arising ability, offering them an opportunity to acquire perceivability, construct organizations, and secure worthwhile agreements with top offices and brands. Trying models, frequently at the beginning phases of their professions, take part in these contests to speed up their way to progress.

The configuration of demonstrating contests differs, yet there are normal components that describe a significant number of these occasions. Normally, displaying challenges include a progression of rounds or difficulties that test various parts of a model's true capacity, including their runway abilities, visual abilities, flexibility, and impressive skill. While the particulars of every rivalry might vary, they by and large offer key ascribes.

Tryouts and Projecting Calls:

Demonstrating rivalries frequently start with open tryouts or projecting calls, where hopeful models have the open door to grandstand their ability and establish an underlying connection. These tryouts act as the section point for competitors, and they are generally held in significant urban communities, permitting members from various districts to join in.

Determination and End Rounds:

When the tryouts are finished, chose competitors continue on toward the principal rivalry adjusts. These rounds regularly incorporate difficulties that reflect the requests of the displaying business. Hopefuls might be evaluated in view of their runway strolls, presenting skills, and by and large presence. The serious idea of these rounds frequently prompts disposals, with judges choosing a more modest gathering of models to progress.

Mentorship and Preparing:

In many displaying rivalries, hopefuls get mentorship and preparing from industry specialists and experienced models. This mentorship remembers direction for runway procedures, presenting, cosmetics application, and styling. Mentorship can be an extraordinary part of the opposition, assisting hopefuls with working on their abilities and certainty.

Photoshoots and Difficulties:

Contests frequently highlight photoshoot moves that survey a model's capacity to work before the camera. These photoshoots may include different subjects, styling, and areas, testing the flexibility and imagination of candidates. At times, models may likewise confront difficulties connected with acting, spontaneous creation, or public talking.

Judging and Criticism:

A board of judges, comprising of industry experts, photographic artists, originators, and different specialists, assess the challengers in each round. Passes judgment on offer input on a model's exhibition, giving experiences and productive analysis. This input is a significant part of the growing experience, assisting challengers with refining their abilities and adjust to the business' requests.

Disposals and Headways:

All through the opposition, models are continuously dispensed with in view of their presentation in the different difficulties and rounds. The quantity of candidates wanes as the opposition advances, eventually prompting a last determination of victors or top-setting models. These finalists frequently get prizes, agreements, or potential chances to work with lofty offices and brands.

Public Democratic and Watcher Commitment:

In some demonstrating contests, watchers and the public assume a part in deciding the victors. This contribution might appear as internet casting a ballot, where the crowd can decide in favor of their #1 hopefuls. Watcher commitment and backing can essentially influence a model's excursion in the opposition.

Terrific Finale and Runway Show:

Displaying rivalries commonly finish in a terrific finale occasion or runway show, where the leftover contenders seek the top positions. This occasion is frequently gone to by industry experts, big names, and design fans. The stupendous finale is a chance for models to feature their development and advancement all through the opposition.

The meaning of demonstrating contests in the design business couldn't possibly be more significant. These occasions act as important stages for finding new ability, advancing variety and inclusivity, and reshaping the business' principles of magnificence. The openness and valuable open doors given by demonstrating challenges can be extraordinary for arising models, pushing them into the spotlight and opening ways to a scope of conceivable outcomes.

One of the most notorious and powerful demonstrating rivalries is the Portage Models Supermodel of the World challenge. Sent off in 1983 by the eminent Passage Models organization, this opposition has found and sent off the professions of a few supermodels, including Alessandra Ambrosio, Adriana Lima, and Chanel Iman. The opposition is known for its worldwide reach, as it scouts ability from nations all over the planet.

The meaning of displaying rivalries stretches out past individual achievement; it influences the business' qualities and practices. Many displaying challenges have embraced variety and inclusivity, pushing for the portrayal of models from different foundations, body types, and identities. These challenges have added to a more comprehensive and delegate displaying world, testing obsolete magnificence standards.

Besides, demonstrating rivalries have been instrumental in advancing moral practices and mindful obtaining inside the design business. Architects and brands related with these challenges frequently line up with economical and moral design works on, setting models for the business to follow. These rivalries are tied in with distinguishing top models as well as about advancing moral and maintainable qualities.

The effect of demonstrating contests stretches out to the displaying organizations that address the champs and finalists. Top demonstrating organizations frequently check out the competitors and champs, offering them agreements and valuable chances to work with high-profile clients. These organizations assume a significant part in sustaining the professions of models, getting appointments, and arranging contracts for their benefit.

Lately, the advanced age has changed the displaying rivalry scene. Virtual entertainment, internet casting a ballot, and computerized stages have intensified the scope and effect of these occasions. Many displaying challenges currently consolidate online commitment, permitting watchers to follow competitors' excursions, partake in casting a ballot, and cooperate with the opposition through different computerized channels.

The worldwide reach of the demonstrating business and the interconnectedness of the computerized age have led to another type of displaying challenges. Web based demonstrating contests have acquired ubiquity, offering a stage for arising models to exhibit their abilities and earn respect without the requirement for actual tryouts and occasions. These virtual challenges influence the force of innovation to find ability from all edges of the world.

While displaying contests offer various open doors, they are not without their difficulties. The extreme and cutthroat nature of these occasions can be sincerely burdening for members. The strain to fulfill industry guidelines, succeed in difficulties, and secure the top positions can prompt pressure and tension. Models might encounter self-uncertainty and vulnerability as they explore the eccentric idea of the opposition.

Also, the public part of displaying rivalries, including public democratic and online commitment, can open competitors to both help and analysis. While public help can be engaging, negative input and online analysis can influence a model's confidence and mental prosperity. It is fundamental for challengers to foster versatility and the ability to understand anyone on a profound level to adapt to the close to home requests of the opposition.

The transient and unusual nature of the demonstrating calling is likewise reflected in displaying rivalries. Challengers might have to adjust to various areas, conditions, and working circumstances all through the opposition. This requires adaptability and the capacity to flourish in different settings.

The coaching and preparing presented during demonstrating contests can be a blade that cuts both ways. While mentorship gives important direction and learning open doors, models should likewise keep up with their validness and singularity. Finding some kind of harmony between adjusting to industry assumptions and remaining consistent with one's exceptional character can be a difficult part of the opposition.

The fact that contestants should explore makes the strain to get appointments and agreements another perspective. While winning a demonstrating contest is a critical accomplishment, it doesn't ensure an effective and persevering through vocation in the business. Models should keep on showing off their abilities in the exceptionally cutthroat universe of style and demonstrating.

The assumptions and difficulties looked by models in the design and displaying industry are reflected in demonstrating rivalries. These occasions are a microcosm of the business, offering arising gifts an opportunity to encounter the requests, energy, and intricacies of the calling. The excursion through tryouts, choice rounds, mentorship, photoshoot difficulties, and ends reflects the genuine encounters of models in the business.

3.2. Themed Photo Shoots and Runway Walks

Inside the domain of design and demonstrating, photograph shoots and runway strolls are two quintessential viewpoints that characterize a model's profession. These exercises permit models to feature their flexibility, imagination, and versatility, whether it's before a camera or on a live runway. In this investigation of themed photograph shoots and runway strolls, we dig into the complexities of these fundamental parts of the demonstrating calling, offering bits of knowledge into their importance, the imaginative difficulties they present, and the ranges of abilities expected to succeed.

Themed Photograph Shoots:

1. **Imaginative Articulation:**
   Themed photograph shoots are a type of imaginative articulation that permits models, photographic artists, and beauticians to team up in recounting a visual story. These shoots frequently rotate around a particular idea, story, or topic, giving an open door to creative investigation. Models are entrusted with encapsulating the embodiment of the topic, interpreting it through their stances, articulations, and association with the climate and props.

2. **Flexibility and Versatility:**
   One of the key abilities that models should have is the capacity to adjust to different subjects and ideas. Themed photograph shoots challenge models to step into various jobs, styles, and states of mind. They might wind up amidst a high-design publication shoot one day and an eccentric, ethereal shoot the following.

This flexibility is a demonstration of a model's reach and impressive skill.

3. **Presenting and Non-verbal communication:**
   Themed photograph gives request a profound comprehension of presenting and non-verbal communication. Models should have the option to pass the mind-set and story of the subject on through their genuineness. The point of a hand, the curve of a back, or the slant of the head can all convey various feelings and stories. Presenting dominance is a key expertise for models in these settings.

4. **Cooperation and Correspondence:**
   The outcome of a themed photograph shoot depends on viable cooperation and correspondence between the model, photographic artist, beautician, and the whole innovative group. Models need to comprehend and decipher the photographic artist's vision, while likewise presenting their imaginative information. Clear correspondence is fundamental to guarantee that everybody is in total agreement in regards to the subject's execution.

5. **Closet and Styling:**
   Themed photograph shoots frequently include elaborate closet and styling decisions. Models might be expected to wear exceptional and on occasion excessive outfits that line up with the subject. The capacity to exemplify the personality of the subject while conveying these outfits with effortlessness and certainty is a demonstration of a model's incredible skill.

6. **Area and Climate:**
   Photograph shoots can occur in various areas and conditions, from studio settings to colorful open air districts. Models should adjust to the circumstances and environmental factors, frequently managing testing climate, territory, or lighting. The capacity to work consistently in different conditions is an important expertise.

7. **Narrating and Feeling:**
   Themed photograph shoots are not just about pausing dramatically; they are tied in with narrating and summoning feeling. Models should associate with the subject on a close to home level and pass that association on through their looks. Whether it's catching the show of a Gothic sentiment or the fun loving nature of a retro-themed shoot, models assume an essential part in deciphering the story.

8. **Cosmetics and Hair:**
   The cosmetics and hair styling for themed photograph shoots can be profoundly specific. Models might go through sensational changes to line up with the subject, expecting them to adjust to unpredictable or intense cosmetics and hair decisions. Models should likewise comprehend how to function with cosmetics specialists and beauticians to accomplish the ideal look.

9. **Variation to Patterns and Styles:**
   Design is consistently advancing, and themed photograph shoots frequently reflect latest things and styles. Models should keep awake to-date with the most popular trend developments and adjust their abilities to suit the contemporary inclinations of the business. Having the option to consistently progress between various styles is a demonstration of a model's attractiveness.

10. **Impressive skill and Tolerance:**

Themed photograph shoots can be intricate and tedious undertakings. Models are supposed to keep up with impressive skill and persistence in the interim, which might include extended periods, numerous outfit changes, and fastidious scrupulousness. Being dependable, reliable, and versatile is significant in these settings.

Runway Strolls:

1. **Balance and Certainty:**
   The runway is a definitive stage for models to show balance and

certainty. A solid and guaranteed runway walk is fundamental. Models ought to ooze self-assuredness and a feeling of control as they drop down the runway, catching the consideration of the crowd and cameras.

2. **Runway Styles:**

There are different runway styles, including the work of art and exquisite runway walk, the high-energy and dynamic runway walk, and the vanguard and dramatic runway walk. The picked style ought to line up with the originator's vision and the idea of the design show. Models should be flexible and equipped for adjusting to various runway styles.

3. **Accuracy and Timing:**

The accuracy and timing of a runway walk are basic. Models should synchronize their stroll with the beat of the music and the movement of the show. The capacity to keep up with steady pacing and dividing, in any event, while strolling in a gathering, is a demonstration of a model's impressive skill.

4. **Body Stance and Development:**

Runway strolls expect models to have perfect body act and controlled developments. This incorporates keeping a straight stance, loosened up shoulders, a sure look, and a liquid step. A model's developments ought to be smooth and easy, conveying effortlessness and tastefulness.

5. **Turn and Turn Procedures:**

Runway strolls frequently include turns and turns, where models grandstand various points of the attire. Models should execute these turns with accuracy and certainty. Turning methods might shift relying upon the design show's style and the fashioner's inclinations.

6. **Transformation to Various Pieces of clothing:**

Models might have to stroll in a large number of pieces of clothing, from voluminous outfits to fitted suits and vanguard manifestations. Adjusting their stroll to suit the qualities of the outfit, like its weight, length, and style, is significant. Models should make each article of clothing look easily sleek and agreeable.

7. **Communicating the Creator's Vision:**

The runway walk is a chance for models to communicate the originator's vision and the embodiment of the assortment. Models should grasp the account and motivation behind the assortment and pass it on through their walk and presence. This arrangement between the model and planner's vision is essential.

8. **Movement and Practice:**

Numerous runway shows include movement and practices. Models should be persevering in their readiness, going to practices, and adhering to the choreographer's directions. The capacity to adjust to arranged schedules and execute them faultlessly is a pivotal part of runway execution.

9. **Incredible skill and Flexibility:**

Models should be proficient and versatile in the quick moving and frequently high-pressure climate of design shows. They might experience startling changes, like latest possible moment outfit adjustments or modifications to the show's structure. Being adaptable and obliging is essential in these circumstances.

10. **Certainty on the Stage:**

At last, runway strolls are a presentation on a stupendous stage. Models should ooze certainty and magnetism, spellbinding the crowd, photographic artists, and industry experts. Certainty isn't just about strolling yet in addition about possessing the stage and making an enduring impression.

Themed photograph shoots and runway strolls are the two powerful mainstays of a model's vocation, offering potential open doors for creative articulation, narrating, and exhibiting flexibility. These exercises require a large number of abilities, from presenting and non-verbal communication to flexibility and incredible skill.

In the realm of themed photograph shoots, models change into characters and exemplify the pith of different topics. They should team up with an inventive group to rejuvenate the subject, interfacing with the story and passing feeling on through their demeanors and postures. Models likewise explore the difficulties of adjusting to various conditions, closet decisions, and styles.

On the runway, models become the living encapsulations of a creator's vision. They should show balance, certainty, and accuracy as they stroll down the catwalk. The runway walk includes different styles and methods, and models need to adjust to the qualities of various articles of clothing. The capacity to communicate the planner's vision and perform arranged schedules with incredible skill is fundamental.

Themed photograph shoots and runway strolls request a serious level of expertise as well as a profound comprehension of the design business' developing patterns and styles. Models need to remain current and adjust to the business' dynamic scene. These exercises are a festival of imagination, creative joint effort, and the force of show in the realm of style and displaying.

3.3. Creative and High-Pressure Challenges

The universe of design and demonstrating is a domain of imaginativeness, innovativeness, and self-articulation. Notwithstanding, it is likewise a space where experts face a large number of innovative and high-pressure difficulties. These difficulties are vital to the business' dynamic nature, requesting advancement, flexibility, and the capacity to succeed under serious examination. In this investigation of imaginative and high-pressure difficulties, we dig into the complex features of the demonstrating calling, including the requests of publication shoots, the thrill of live design shows, and the careful specialty of magnificence crusades.

Inventive Difficulties:

1. Article Shoots:

Article shoots are the core of style photography, where models and picture takers team up to make outwardly convincing stories. Models are supposed to carry their imagination and distinction to these shoots, frequently working intimately with picture takers to create special accounts. Publication shoots challenge models to exemplify different characters and states of mind, from high-design to cutting edge, and to do as such with realness and creative pizazz.

2. **Typifying the Idea:**

One of the essential imaginative difficulties in article shoots is the capacity to typify the idea or subject of the shoot. Models should submerge themselves in the account, understanding the person they are depicting and conveying the comparing feelings. Whether it's an ethereal pixie in a forest setting or a strong and tense person in a metropolitan climate, models should embrace the quintessence of the idea.

3. **Posture and Development:**

Innovative publication shoots frequently include offbeat and emotional postures and developments. Models are expected to try different things with their genuineness, investigating strange points and articulations. The capacity to convey a feeling of ease and dynamism while keeping an outwardly enamoring organization is an expertise that models should dominate.

4. **Coordinated effort and Imaginativeness:**

Models team up with picture takers, beauticians, cosmetics specialists, and innovative chiefs to rejuvenate the article idea. This cooperative interaction requires a harmony between private creative articulation and adherence to the group's vision. Models should give their imaginative contribution while likewise regarding the commitments of the whole inventive group.

5. **Natural Variation:**

Publication shoots can happen in assorted and frequently testing conditions, from distant normal scenes to clamoring metropolitan roads. Models should adjust to these environmental elements, exploring issues like atmospheric conditions, territory, and accessible lighting. Natural variation is fundamental for the progress of the shoot.

6. **Narrating Through Symbolism:**

In the realm of style photography, models are narrators, utilizing their bodies and articulations to convey accounts and feelings. The test lies in making an interpretation of the story into a visual language, permitting watchers to draw in with the symbolism and associate with the idea on a more profound level.

7. **Adaptability and Reach:**

Models are supposed to exhibit flexibility and an expansive reach in their work. They might be expected to move starting with one person or subject then onto the next flawlessly. The capacity to exhibit various features of their character and style is a demonstration of their imagination and flexibility.

8. **Staying aware of Patterns:**

Design is steadily developing, and models should remain sensitive to the most recent patterns and styles. Monitoring the business' changing inclinations and it is fundamental to adjust to contemporary creative developments. Models need to constantly develop their imaginative way to deal with stay applicable.

9. **Close to home Reverberation:**

Interfacing with the crowd on a close to home level is a critical inventive test. Models should convey feelings that reverberate with watchers, whether it's a feeling of secret, bliss, sexiness, or defiance. The capacity to bring out certifiable feelings in the crowd is a characteristic of a model's imaginativeness.

High-Tension Difficulties:

1. **Live Style Shows:**

Style shows are thrilling and high-pressure occasions where models walk live on the runway, displaying assortments before a live crowd, cameras, and industry experts. The strain to perform perfectly in a live setting, with no space for retakes, can be extraordinary. Models should execute exact runway strolls, timing, and movement, while keeping up with balance and certainty.

2. **Accuracy and Timing:**
Live design shows request outright accuracy and timing. Models should synchronize their stroll with the music, the movement, and the lighting, guaranteeing that they hit their imprints definitively. A minor slip up can disturb the whole progression of the show.

3. **Numerous Changes:**
Design shows frequently include numerous outfit changes. Models might have to change starting with one outfit then onto the next in no time, all while keeping a cool head and runway-prepared appearance. The behind the stage free for all of speedy changes adds to the high-pressure climate.

4. **Adjusting to Different Runway Styles:**
Different design shows might include shifting runway styles, from exemplary and exquisite to cutting edge and dynamic. Models need to adjust to these styles, guaranteeing that their runway walk lines up with the originator's vision and the idea of the show. Flexibility is fundamental.

5. **Crowd and Industry Consideration:**
The runway is a phase that gathers huge consideration from both the crowd and industry experts. Models are under steady examination, with planners, specialists, photographic artists, and style aficionados evaluating their presentation. The capacity to order the stage and enamor the crowd is a high-pressure challenge.

6. **Taking care of Last-Minute Changes:**
Style shows can be eccentric, with latest possible moment changes in the setup, movement, or outfits. Models should stay versatile and made in the face out of these surprising changes. Keeping up with amazing skill and certainty is crucial.

7. **Resisting the urge to panic Under Tension:**
   The adrenaline and strain of live design shows can overpower. Models should figure out how to hold their nerves in line and perform with beauty and certainty. Keeping a feeling of quiet under tension is an expertise that creates with experience.

8. **Dismissals and Investigate:**
   The displaying business is profoundly serious, and models might confront dismissals and evaluate. Few out of every odd projecting outcomes in a booking, and models should figure out how to adapt to dismissal and keep up with their inspiration. Productive analysis is a fundamental part of expert development.

9. **Consistent Improvement:**
   Models are feeling the squeeze to improve and refine their abilities. The opposition is furious, and the business' norms are steadily advancing. Models need to remain focused on continuous personal growth, whether it's through runway instructing, presenting practice, or profound strength preparing.

10. **Meeting Industry Assumptions:**

The high-pressure difficulties in the business spin around meeting and surpassing industry assumptions. Models are supposed to keep a specific degree of impressive skill, versatility, and attractiveness. Living up to these assumptions is an everyday responsibility.

Imaginative and high-pressure difficulties in the style and demonstrating industry are a demonstration of the calling's dynamic and cut-throat nature. Models are specialists as well as entertainers, expected to convey faultless exhibitions in both imaginative and live settings.

Themed photograph shoots request imagination, abilities to narrate, and the expertise to adjust to assorted conditions, subjects, and styles. Models work together with innovative groups to rejuvenate visual stories, associating with the crowd on a profound level. The test lies in offsetting individual creative articulation with the vision of the group and the business' consistently evolving patterns.

Live style shows carry models to the middle stage, where accuracy, timing, and flexibility are fundamental. The strain to perform completely in a live setting, under the full concentrations eyes of industry experts and design devotees, can be thrilling and overwhelming. Models should stay totally under control, certainty, and balance while executing exact runway strolls and numerous outfit changes.

Meeting the high-pressure difficulties in the displaying business requires ceaseless personal development, flexibility, and versatility. Models need to stay aware of advancing industry assumptions and remain significant in a consistently evolving scene. Scrutinize and dismissal are essential for the excursion, however they act as any open doors for development and advancement.

In the realm of style and demonstrating, it isn't just about looking lovely; it is tied in with conveying immaculate exhibitions and making an interpretation of imaginative ideas into enthralling symbolism and live encounters. The imaginative and high-pressure difficulties models face are not deterrents; they are venturing stones to progress and persevering through vocations in the business.

Chapter Four

Triumphs and Struggles

In the domain of design and displaying, wins and battles are different sides of a similar runway. The excursion of a model is a story of desire, strength, and the quest for progress, interweaved with the difficulties, dismissals, and the challenging move to the top. In this investigation of wins and battles, we dig into the complex features of the displaying calling, divulging the snapshots of magnificence, the impediments that models defy, and the flexibility that impels them forward.

Wins:

1. **Handling the Principal Gig:**
   The excursion for a hopeful model frequently starts with the victorious snapshot of handling their most memorable displaying gig. This advancement might come after various tryouts and dismissals, making it a groundbreaking event that denotes the beginning of their expert profession. The energy and feeling of achievement that follow are remarkable.

2. **The Main Runway Show:**
   Venturing onto the runway without precedent for a live style

show is a characterizing win in a model's excursion. The invigoration of exhibiting an originator's assortment, the splendid lights, and the sound of praise from the crowd make an euphoric second. It's a summit of long stretches of difficult work and devotion.

3. **Marking with a Top Organization:**
   One of the main victories for a model is marking with an esteemed demonstrating organization. Being perceived and addressed by a famous organization is a demonstration of their true capacity and attractiveness. It opens ways to a universe of chances, from high-profile appointments to worldwide agreements.

4. **Handling a Sought after Magazine Cover:**
   A sought after magazine cover is an achievement in a model's vocation. It addresses acknowledgment and unmistakable quality in the design business. From Vogue to Elle, gracing the front of a lofty design distribution is a victory that moves a model into the spotlight.

5. **Worldwide Achievement:**
   Breaking into the worldwide demonstrating scene is a wonderful victory. Models who secure worldwide agreements and work with famous originators and brands on a worldwide scale experience a brilliant ascent in their vocations. This accomplishment is a demonstration of their ability and flexibility.

6. **High-Profile Coordinated efforts:**
   Working together with high-profile originators, picture takers, and brands is a victory that hoists a model's status in the business. It might include working with famous fashioners like Chanel or Dior, shooting with incredible photographic artists, or turning into the substance of an extravagance brand. Such joint efforts are a stamp of acknowledgment.

7. **Accomplishing Supermodel Status:**
   Turning into a supermodel, an uncommon and first class status in the displaying scene, is a profession characterizing win. Supermodels are notable figures, known for their effect on design,

excellence, and culture. Accomplishing this status implies being perceived universally and lastingly affecting the business.

8. **Variety and Inclusivity Support:**
Win in the demonstrating business isn't restricted to individual achievement. Models who utilize their foundation to advocate for variety, inclusivity, and moral practices contribute fundamentally to positive change in the business. Turning into a voice for change and testing obsolete magnificence standards is a victory by its own doing.

9. **Supporting Mentorship:**
Mentorship assumes a urgent part in a model's excursion. Being coached by industry veterans and supermodels is a victory that offers significant direction and speeds up a model's development. These mentorship connections add to the improvement of a model's abilities and impressive skill.

10. **Proficient Development and Life span:**

The capacity to keep a flourishing profession throughout the long term, adjusting to changing industry drifts and staying important, is a victory in itself. Models who accomplish proficient development and life span in the business exhibit flexibility and versatility.

While wins are the snapshots of festivity and accomplishment in a model's excursion, they are much of the time joined by their reasonable portion of battles. These battles are the difficulties, dismissals, and impediments that models should explore as they seek after their fantasies in the wildly serious universe of design and displaying.

Battles:

1. **Dismissal and Projecting Disappointments:**
One of the most well-known battles for models is confronting dismissal during projecting calls and tryouts. Models might go to various castings without getting a booking. Dismissal is a steady

presence in the business, and models should figure out how to adapt to it and keep up with their inspiration.

2. **Serious Rivalry:**

The displaying business is exceptionally cutthroat, with countless hopeful models competing for a predetermined number of chances. The strain to stick out and succeed in a soaked field is a repetitive battle. Models should consistently improve their abilities and foster a one of a kind selling point.

3. **Industry Excellence Principles:**

The business' customary excellence principles have been a longstanding battle, with models frequently forced to adjust to explicit rules. The strain to keep a specific body size, shape, or look can genuinely burden. Splitting away from these norms and pushing for variety is a continuous test.

4. **Close to home Versatility:**

Displaying is a calling that requests profound versatility. The tensions of the business, dismissals, and the need to keep up with fearlessness can negatively affect a model's psychological prosperity. Creating profound strength is a constant excursion for models.

5. **Arduous Work Conditions:**

Models oftentimes work in requesting and flighty circumstances, from extended periods on set to shoots in testing conditions. The physical and profound requests of the calling can be exhausting, trying a model's perseverance and flexibility.

6. **Adjusting Individual and Expert Life:**

Adjusting individual and expert life can be a battle, as the displaying calling frequently includes travel and sporadic timetables. Keeping up with connections, side interests, and individual prosperity while chasing after a displaying profession is a consistent test.

7. **Moral Worries:**

Models frequently face moral worries connected with the business, for example, the treatment of models on set, manageability rehearses, and capable obtaining. Upholding for moral guidelines and supportability is a fight that a few models decide to take on.

8. **Public Investigation and Online Entertainment Strain:**
In the time of web-based entertainment, models are under consistent public examination. Pessimistic remarks, online analysis, and the strain to keep an organized web-based picture can sincerely challenge. Models should foster systems to adapt to the advanced spotlight.

9. **Conflicting Pay:**
The demonstrating calling is known for its conflicting pay. Models might encounter monetary vulnerability, with times of high income followed by calmer times. Monetary steadiness and arranging are continuous battles for some models.

10. **Remaining Important and Versatile:**

Remaining pertinent in an industry that continually develops is a test. Models should adjust to changing style, mechanical advances, and moving industry standards. This requires progressing learning and improvement.

Wins and battles are two features of the demonstrating venture, joined in the texture of a model's vocation. Wins are the snapshots of triumph, acknowledgment, and effect. They address the zenith of difficult work, commitment, and ability. Battles, then again, are the snags, dismissals, and difficulties that models stand up to on their way to progress.

Wins are the milestones of a model's excursion, from the thrilling first gig to the global leap forward and high-profile joint efforts. Accomplishing supermodel status and utilizing the stage to advocate for change are great victories that characterize a model's inheritance. Wins are the snapshots of festivity and acknowledgment of dreams.

Battles are the obstacles that models face all through their professions. They incorporate dismissals, serious contest, the strain to adjust to industry excellence principles, and the requirement for profound strength. Models likewise wrestle with difficult work conditions, adjusting individual and expert life, moral worries, and the difficulties of remaining significant in a unique industry. Battles are the trial of a model's assurance and flexibility.

The demonstrating calling is an excursion of steadiness and versatility. Models figure out how to explore the always developing design industry, drawing strength from their victories and involving their battles as venturing stones toward their objectives. Wins and battles are the indistinguishable mates in the demonstrating odyssey, forming the encounters and character of models as they pursue their fantasies under the brilliant lights of the design world.

4.1. Successes and Milestones

In the domain of design and demonstrating, victories and achievements are the venturing stones that clear the way to a fulfilling and persevering through profession. The excursion of a model is set apart by snapshots of accomplishment, acknowledgment, and self-awareness. In this investigation of victories and achievements, we dive into the complex features of the demonstrating calling, uncovering the milestones that characterize a model's heritage and mirror their excursion of commitment and assurance.

Triumphs:

1. **Displaying Agreements with Top Organizations:**
   Protecting agreements with top demonstrating organizations is perhaps the earliest significant progress in a model's vocation. It connotes acknowledgment and approval by industry specialists. These offices give models fundamental direction, backing, and admittance to lofty open doors.

2. **Global Appointments and Travel:**
   Booking global gigs and leaving on demonstrating tasks all over the planet is a huge accomplishment for models. It exhibits their worldwide allure and attractiveness. These encounters offer

openness to different societies, style scenes, and open doors for systems administration.

3. **High-Profile Missions:**

Landing high-profile crusades with eminent brands is a demonstration of a model's attractiveness and flexibility. Lobbies for extravagance design houses, excellence items, and way of life marks frequently earn huge consideration and perceivability.

4. **Runway Wins:**

Wins on the runway, for example, featuring style shows or strolling for renowned planners during significant design weeks, are vital turning points in a model's vocation. These encounters support a model's standing as well as give admittance to a wide crowd of style fans and industry experts.

5. **Magazine Covers and Publications:**

Gracing the front of design magazines and being highlighted in publication spreads is a sign of a fruitful displaying profession. It means the model's effect on the business and their impact on style. Magazine covers are frequently famous and desired.

6. **Supermodel Status:**

Accomplishing supermodel status is a surprising outcome in the demonstrating scene. Supermodels are notable figures known for their otherworldly impact on design, magnificence, and culture. The title accompanies tremendous acknowledgment, potential open doors, and an enduring heritage.

7. **Promotion and Magnanimity:**

Models who utilize their foundation for promotion and magnanimous endeavors make progress past their professions. They become voices for change, resolving issues like variety, inclusivity, maintainability, and social causes. This achievement mirrors a promise to having a beneficial outcome.

8. **Undertakings:**

A few models adventure into business, sending off their own style lines, excellence items, or way of life brands. The progress of these undertakings grandstands a model's pioneering keenness and capacity to grow their impact past the runway.

9. **Self-improvement and Strength:**
   Self-improvement and strength are victories that frequently go unnoticed. Models who develop, foster profound strength, and keep an identity in the midst of the difficulties of the business accomplish a huge degree of outcome in their own lives.

10. **Life span and Heritage:**

The capacity to support a flourishing profession throughout the long term, adjusting to changing industry drifts and staying pertinent, is a sign of outcome in the demonstrating scene. A model's inheritance is worked through their persevering through influence on the business and culture.

Achievements:

1. **First Photoshoot:**
   The primary expert photoshoot marks an achievement in a model's excursion. It addresses the change from a hopeful model to a functioning proficient. This achievement frequently happens with an arising picture taker or for a neighborhood project.

2. **Runway Introduction:**
   Strolling in one's most memorable design show, particularly during a nearby or local occasion, is a characterizing achievement. It offers a brief look into the elements of live design shows and the energy of the runway.

3. **Neighborhood and Public Openness:**
   Acquiring openness inside one's neighborhood or public design scene is a basic achievement. It might include showing up in nearby magazines, taking part in territorial style weeks, and building a presence in the homegrown design industry.

4. **Acknowledgment by Arising Creators:**
   Creators who are beginning their professions frequently work

together with arising models. Being perceived and picked by arising fashioners is an essential achievement for models hoping to construct a portfolio and organization inside the business.

5. **Worldwide Disclosure:**

For models looking for worldwide acknowledgment, the snapshot of being found or welcome to work abroad is a stupendous achievement. It denotes the start of a worldwide excursion.

6. **Significant Style Weeks:**

Strolling in significant style weeks, like New York, Paris, Milan, or London, is a sought after achievement for models. It gives openness to the worldwide style tip top and makes way for bigger accomplishments.

7. **Runway Opens for Top Fashioners:**

At the point when top originators and design houses stretch out solicitations to models to stroll in their shows, an achievement addresses industry affirmation and recognition. These creators frequently set the vibe for style and styles.

8. **Signature Missions:**

Landing mark crusades with laid out brands denotes an achievement. These missions, frequently portrayed by long haul organizations, address a model's interesting allure and persevering through influence on a brand's picture.

9. **Humanitarian Drives:**

At the point when models take part in magnanimity and utilize their foundation for social causes, it denotes an achievement in their profession. Support and adding to a more prominent great become a huge piece of their inheritance.

10. **Life span and Reexamination:**

Accomplishing a long and effective profession while rehashing oneself to stay significant is an achievement that mirrors a model's versatility, flexibility, and capacity to explore the business' development.

The demonstrating calling is an excursion of desire, commitment, and wins. Victories are the snapshots of festivity and acknowledgment in a model's vocation, from getting top organization agreements to accomplishing supermodel status. These triumphs are many times the aftereffect of long stretches of difficult work, flexibility, and devotion.

Achievements are the markers along the way, from the first photoshoot to acknowledgment by arising creators, to strolling in significant style weeks, lastly to getting through progress and self-improvement. Achievements address the advancement and improvement of a model's profession, forming their experience and industry standing.

A model's process is a nonstop pattern of taking a stab at progress, commending achievements, and confronting difficulties. Victories and achievements are the prizes and acknowledgments that models procure through their steady quest for greatness in a dynamic and serious industry. They characterize the tradition of a model, mirroring the effect they leave on the design world and then some.

4.2. The Emotional Rollercoaster

The universe of style and displaying isn't simply about pausing dramatically and wearing stylish ensembles; an industry gives models an interesting profound rollercoaster. The calling is a confusing mix of elating ups and unsettling downs, where the excursion is as much an investigation of internal strength and self-disclosure for all intents and purposes about outer appearances. In this investigation of the close to home rollercoaster, we dive into the many-sided features of the displaying calling, revealing the serious feelings that models insight and the procedures they utilize to explore the profound scene.

The Highs:

1. **Delight of Achievement:**

   Quite possibly of the most thrilling high in a model's vocation is the rapture that follows achievement. This could be handling a sought after demonstrating contract, gracing the front of a lofty style magazine, or strolling the runway for a prestigious creator. The feeling of achievement, acknowledgment, and the information that long stretches of difficult work have paid off is euphoric.

2. **Runway Wins:**

Strolling down the runway, with the crowd's eyes fixed on a model, can a rush high. The acclaim, the lights, and the adventure of exhibiting originator manifestations are charging. Featuring a significant design show or getting a heartfelt applause from the crowd are minutes that make a flood of adrenaline.

3. **Magazine Covers and Articles:**

Being chosen for a magazine cover or publication spread is a high point in a model's vocation. It isn't just about the notoriety of the distribution however the valuable chance to be the essence of a style, impacting style and culture. These accomplishments are praised with delight and pride.

4. **Global Acknowledgment:**

Earning global respect and being reserved for high-profile gigs in various regions of the planet is a high that mirrors a model's worldwide allure. It opens ways to a different scope of encounters, societies, and open doors, prompting a more extensive organization and raised vocation status.

5. **Backing and Social Effect:**

Models who utilize their foundation for backing and social effect experience close to home highs that reach out past their professions. The feeling of rolling out a good improvement and impacting cultural standards can significantly satisfy. Models frequently become advocates for variety, inclusivity, maintainability, and magnanimity, making a feeling of direction.

6. **Snapshots of Self-awareness:**

Self-awareness and self-disclosure are close to home highs that frequently slip through the cracks. The capacity to explore the inner difficulties of the business, construct versatility, and foster a healthy identity in the midst of the disorder of style weeks and it is a huge high to request plans.

7. **Mentorship and Directing Others:**
Encountering the satisfaction of directing and coaching yearning models, assisting them with defeating deterrents and accomplish their fantasies, can sincerely remunerate. Models who take on mentorship jobs track down delight in supporting the up and coming age of ability.

8. **Seeking after Inventive Endeavors:**

A few models investigate innovative endeavors past their displaying professions, for example, style plan, business, or creative pursuits. These endeavors offer a feeling of artistic liberty and accomplishment.

The Lows:

1. **Dismissal and Projecting Disappointments:**
Dismissal is an inborn piece of the displaying calling. For each effective booking, models might confront different dismissals at projecting calls. Managing dismissal and the close to home cost it takes can cripple.

2. **Extraordinary Contest:**
The profoundly serious nature of the displaying business can prompt insecurities and self-question. Models continually contrast themselves with others, which can genuinely burden.

3. **Industry Excellence Guidelines:**
The strain to adjust to industry excellence guidelines, frequently based on body size, shape, and appearance, can prompt self-perception issues and profound trouble. Attempting to keep a specific look can bring about pressure and gloomy feelings.

4. **Close to home Strength:**
The profound strength expected in the business, while a high point, can likewise be a low in snapshots of weakness. Overseeing

dismissal, analysis, and the tensions of the style world can genuinely deplete.

5. **Exhausting Work Conditions:**

The truly requesting and erratic work conditions in the demonstrating calling can negatively affect a model's physical and profound prosperity. Extended periods, travel, and the need to adjust to different conditions can debilitate.

6. **Adjusting Individual and Expert Life:**

Keeping a balance between fun and serious activities can be a battle for models, who frequently need to travel widely and work sporadic hours. The close to home cost of being away from friends and family or passing up private occasions can challenge.

7. **Moral Worries:**

Moral worries, for example, the treatment of models on set, supportability rehearses, and dependable obtaining, can sincerely trouble. Upholding for moral norms frequently includes facing industry rehearses.

8. **Public Examination and Virtual Entertainment Tension:**

In the time of virtual entertainment, models are under consistent public examination. Pessimistic remarks, online analysis, and the strain to keep an organized internet based picture can sincerely challenge. The close to home effect of online judgment can be significant.

9. **Conflicting Pay:**

The demonstrating calling is known for its conflicting pay. Models might encounter monetary vulnerability, with times of high profit followed by calmer times. Monetary strength and arranging are continuous difficulties for some models.

10. **Remaining Significant and Versatile:**

Remaining significant in an industry that continually develops is a test that requires progressing learning, versatility, and the profound status to embrace change.

The profound rollercoaster of the displaying calling is a consistent transition between the highs of progress and the lows of difficulties and close to home battles. It is an industry where outside accomplishments frequently accompany close to home expenses, and the capacity to explore these profound high points and low points is a demonstration of a model's versatility.

Models frequently foster different techniques to explore the close to home rollercoaster:

1. **Taking care of oneself:** Models focus on taking care of oneself to keep up with their profound prosperity. This incorporates actual activity, contemplation, skincare, and psychological well-being rehearses.

2. **Emotionally supportive networks:** areas of strength for building frameworks with companions, family, and coaches assists models with adapting to inner difficulties and celebrate victories.

3. **Looking for Proficient Assistance:** A few models look for the direction of psychological well-being experts to deal with the close to home cost of the business.

4. **Support and Strengthening:** Models utilize their foundation to advocate for positive change in the business, resolving issues like body energy, variety, manageability, and moral guidelines.

5. **Versatility Preparing:** Creating close to home strength is a fundamental expertise for models, and many take part in flexibility preparing to adapt to the requests of the calling.

6. **Adjusting Individual and Expert Life:** Tracking down ways of adjusting individual and expert life is pivotal for close to home strength.

The close to home rollercoaster of the displaying calling is both a test and a wellspring of self-improvement. It is an excursion of self-revelation, self-acknowledgment, and tracking down reason past the excitement and style of the design world.

The universe of style and displaying is a complex industry, one that offers models a novel close to home rollercoaster ride. The ups and downs, the snapshots of accomplishment and the difficulties confronted, all in all characterize the profound scene of the calling. Models explore this rollercoaster with strength, self-improvement, and methodologies for close to home prosperity. It is an industry that shapes outside appearances as well as gives a material to inward flexibility and self-revelation, making the excursion all the really convincing and groundbreaking.

4.3. Relationship Dynamics Among Contestants

In the high-stakes universe of reality displaying rivalries, the elements among contenders assume a urgent part in forming the general insight. These elements include a great many cooperations, from kinships and partnerships to competitions and clashes. The perplexing connections that unfurl in the background are as basic to the account as the actual runway. In this investigation of relationship elements among competitors, we dig into the diverse social scene of displaying rivalries, uncovering the fellowship, rivalry, collusions, and the significant effect these connections have on the challengers' excursions.

1. Friendship and Fellowship:

Hopefuls in demonstrating rivalries frequently structure close bonds with each other. The common encounters, challenges, and the comprehension of the remarkable tensions of the business make a feeling of friendship. These companionships offer consistent reassurance, kinship, and a feeling of having a place in a serious climate.

2. Coalitions and Coordinated efforts:

Vital collusions and coordinated efforts can be a typical methodology among hopefuls. They might shape coalitions to altogether uphold each other in challenges, share data, or help each other explore the complexities of the opposition. Cooperative endeavors can prompt shared victories.

3. Cutthroat Competitions:

Rivalry is at the core of displaying challenges, and it frequently prompts competitions among contenders. These contentions might be brought into the world from a longing to surpass each other, secure a sought after booking, or gain the adjudicators' approval. While cutthroat contentions can be extraordinary, they likewise drive contenders to stretch their boundaries.

4. Proficient Regard:

Hopefuls frequently foster a profound expert regard for each other. They perceive each other's ability and devotion to the specialty. This shared regard can encourage a sound and strong cutthroat climate.

5. Mentorship and Direction:

More experienced challengers might take on mentorship jobs, directing fresher hopefuls through the opposition. They offer exhortation, share industry experiences, and offer profound help. Mentorship connections are based on a groundwork of trust and shared encounters.

6. Inner Difficulties:

The profound rollercoaster of the opposition can prompt snapshots of weakness and personal difficulties. Hopefuls might trust in each other about their battles and look for comfort in shared encounters.

7. Group Difficulties:

A few rivalries consolidate group difficulties that expect competitors to cooperate. These difficulties can either reinforce unions or lead to clashes assuming there are contrasts in assessment or work styles.

8. Heartfelt Snares:

Heartfelt connections among contenders are normal. The closeness, shared interests, and profound force of the opposition can prompt heartfelt ensnarements. These connections may either offer close to home help or bring extra intricacies into the opposition.

9. Clashes and Show:

Clashes, conflicts, and show are regular side-effects of rivalry. They can emerge from contrasts in character, values, or a conflict of self images. While clashes can be troublesome, they likewise add a layer of interest to the opposition's story.

10. The Effect of Disposals:

Disposals can significantly influence the elements among competitors. The flight of an individual contender can set off a scope of feelings, from trouble and compassion to help and expanded rivalry. The elements frequently shift with every end.

Candidates in displaying contests frequently experience a wide range of feelings and connections. These elements shape the general insight, adding profundity and intricacy to the opposition's story. Competitors who explore these connections successfully can use them for their potential benefit, making an emotionally supportive network that improves their excursion.

The Procedures and Results:

1. Vital Partnerships:

Hopefuls may decisively shape partnerships to get an upper hand. By teaming up with others, they can pool assets, share information, and increment their possibilities winning difficulties. These coalitions can stretch out past the opposition, prompting proficient joint efforts after the show.

2. Compromise:

Challengers who succeed in overseeing clashes and conflicts frequently gain appreciation and backing from both their companions and the appointed authorities. Compromise abilities are important in the displaying business, where collaboration and amazing skill are exceptionally respected.

3. Utilizing Mentorship:

Hopefuls who benefit from mentorship frequently experience individual and expert development. They procure industry bits of knowledge, work on their abilities, and foster the close to home strength expected for a demonstrating vocation. Mentorship can fundamentally impact a challenger's excursion.

4. Building a Positive Standing:

Competitors who keep a positive and expert standing all through the opposition will generally earn the regard and backing of their kindred candidates and the adjudicators. This standing can open ways to future open doors in the business.

5. Embracing Profound Weakness:

Hopefuls who are open about their personal difficulties and weaknesses make true associations with their friends and the crowd. Their eagerness to share their battles can make them appealing and charming figures.

6. Exploring Close connections:

Competitors in close connections frequently need to explore the intricacies of adjusting individual and expert elements. The people who effectively deal with these connections keep up with center around their vocation while additionally appreciating consistent reassurance.

7. Strength In the midst of Ends:

Hopefuls who exhibit strength and effortlessness during ends gain the appreciation of their companions and the crowd. These candidates frequently get backing and support from the people who have been wiped out.

8. Adding to Show and Storylines:

Challengers who add to clashes and show might draw consideration and make critical storylines in the opposition. While this can have both positive and negative repercussions, it can build their perceivability and make an enduring effect.

The Development of Connections:

As the opposition advances, connections among competitors frequently develop. The underlying brotherhood might give approach to uplifted competitions as the stakes get higher. Challengers might shape further bonds with the individuals who share their excursion, and mentorship connections might set. The inner difficulties and the encounters of disposals can bring hopefuls closer, encouraging a feeling of fortitude.

In any case, the tensions of the opposition can likewise prompt cracks in connections, with clashes and show escalating. The elements among hopefuls reflect the profound rollercoaster of the opposition, with snapshots of solidarity, pressure, goal, and change.

The Post-Rivalry Effect:

The connections framed during a demonstrating rivalry can lastingly affect a challenger's profession. Contenders who keep up areas of strength for with their companions frequently have an organization of experts they can team up with in the business. Mentorship connections laid out during the opposition can keep on giving direction and backing. Hopefuls who explore clashes and show really may master significant compromise abilities that work well for them in their professions.

The effect of these connections stretches out past the actual opposition. Competitors who keep up with positive notorieties and profound validness frequently fabricate areas of strength for a with the crowd, prompting fan followings and supports. The connections and encounters from the opposition become piece of a competitor's story, adding to their own image and industry standing.

In rundown, the relationship elements among competitors in demonstrating contests are a complicated trap of companionships, coalitions, contentions, mentorships, clashes, and profound associations. These connections are fundamental to the general story of the opposition, adding profundity and interest to the candidates' excursions. Challengers who explore these elements successfully can use them for their potential benefit, making an emotionally supportive network that improves their professions in the dynamic and cutthroat universe of displaying.

Chapter Five

Personal Growth and Transformation

The excursion of a model in the realm of design and demonstrating isn't exclusively about appearances and the glamour of the runway; it is a significant course of self-improvement and change. The difficulties, encounters, and connections inside the business make a pot for self-disclosure, versatility, and improvement. In this investigation of self-improvement and change, we dig into the significant changes that models go through as they explore the intricacies of the displaying calling and how these changes stretch out past the runway to profoundly impact their lives and characters.

The Mission for Self-Revelation:

The excursion of a model starts with a mission for self-revelation. Hopeful models frequently leave on this way to investigate their personalities, abilities, and potential. The demonstrating calling, with its extraordinary mix of inventiveness and discipline, turns into a material for this investigation.

****1. Personality Investigation:**

As models enter the business, they are presented to a different scope of styles, feel, and inventive ideas. They try different things with various looks and personas, prompting a more profound comprehension of their own characters. The business' consolation of independence and uniqueness encourages an identity revelation.

****2. Social Awareness:**

Demonstrating as often as possible includes working with world-wide originators, picture takers, and groups. This opens models to different societies, customs, and points of view. The experience of exploring different social settings encourages social responsiveness and a widened perspective.

****3. Certainty Building:**

One of the main parts of self-awareness in displaying is the advancement of fearlessness. Models figure out how to convey themselves with balance, ooze self-assuredness, and venture a picture of self-conviction. This certainty frequently stretches out to their own lives.

****4. Profound Strength:**

The displaying calling requests profound versatility even with difficulties, dismissals, and the tensions of the business. Models foster the ability to return quickly from misfortunes, adapt to analysis, and keep areas of strength for an of self.

****5. Impressive skill and Flexibility:**

Models are presented to a speedy and steadily evolving industry. They get familiar with the significance of amazing skill, reliability, and flexibility. These abilities benefit their displaying professions as well as upgrade their capacity to prevail in different parts of life.

****6. Monetary Proficiency:**

Exploring the displaying business' conflicting pay designs requires monetary education. Models figure out how to deal with their profit, plan for times of lower pay, and settle on savvy monetary choices.

****7. Support and Charity:**

Self-awareness frequently stretches out to promotion and charity. Models who accomplish self-awareness become advocates for positive change in the business, resolving issues like variety, inclusivity, maintainability, and social causes. They utilize their foundation to have a constructive outcome.

Changing Through Encounters:

Models go through huge changes through their encounters in the business. The powerful idea of the calling, with its high-pressure conditions and different tasks, shapes their own and proficient development.

****1. Imaginative Investigation:**

Working with fashioners, photographic artists, and beauticians permits models to submerge themselves in innovative approaches. They investigate different styles and feel, frequently pushing the limits of their usual ranges of familiarity. This imaginative investigation reaches out past their demonstrating vocations, affecting their own style and creative interests.

****2. Worldwide Openness:**

Global appointments open models to a bunch of societies, dialects, and customs. The capacity to adjust to various conditions and associate with people from assorted foundations improves their own lives and expands their perspectives.

****3. Style and Industry Experiences:**

Models are at the bleeding edge of style and industry experiences. They gain an inside and out comprehension of the design world, which frequently impacts their own style and design decisions.

****4. Systems administration and Relationship Building:**

Building associations with industry experts, from originators and photographic artists to cosmetics craftsmen and beauticians, upgrades a model's social and expert organization. These connections frequently lead to amazing open doors and joint efforts past their demonstrating professions.

****5. The capacity to understand individuals on a profound level:**

The personal difficulties of the business expect models to foster ability to understand individuals on a profound level. They become more sensitive to their own feelings and the feelings of others, encouraging better connections in their own lives.

****6. Flexibility and Versatility:**

Flexibility and versatility are key ascribes models procure. The capacity to quickly return from dismissals and adjust to changing conditions furnishes them with fundamental abilities.

****7. Promotion and Social Effect:**

Models who go through self-awareness frequently become advocates for positive change in the business. They utilize their foundation to resolve issues like variety, inclusivity, supportability, and social causes, diverting their groundbreaking encounters into promotion and charity.

Adjusting Individual and Expert Development:

Offsetting self-awareness with the requests of a demonstrating vocation is a basic part of a model's excursion. The capacity to explore the double liabilities of a high-profile calling and individual prosperity is a demonstration of a model's development and development.

****1. Balance between fun and serious activities:**

Keeping a balance between fun and serious activities can be trying for models, particularly when they need to travel habitually and work sporadic hours. The capacity to focus on private prosperity, connections, and taking care of oneself shows self-improvement.

****2. Connections and Family:**

Models frequently need to oversee connections and family responsibilities close by their professions. The improvement of sound connections and close to home bonds with friends and family is a fundamental part of self-improvement.

****3. Taking care of oneself and Wellbeing:**

Models focus on taking care of oneself and health to support their vocations and individual lives. This incorporates actual wellness, psychological well-being practices, skincare, and unwinding strategies.

****4. Learning and Improvement:**

Models proceed to acquire and foster their abilities all through their vocations. They participate in studios, courses, and personal growth drives, mirroring their obligation to self-improvement.

****5. Monetary Obligation:**

Models frequently handle fluctuating wages, making monetary obligation a critical part of self-awareness. The capacity to oversee funds, plan for the future, and pursue informed choices adds to by and large prosperity.

The Enduring Effect:

The self-awareness and change that models experience have an enduring effect that reaches out past their vocations. These changes shape their lives, connections, and the heritage they leave in the business.

****1. Validness and Strengthening:**

Models who go through self-awareness frequently become advocates for realness and strengthening. They utilize their foundation to urge others to embrace their distinction, trust in themselves, and have a constructive outcome.

****2. Effect on Industry Practices:**

Models who advocate for positive change frequently impact industry rehearses. They challenge obsolete excellence standards, advance variety and inclusivity, and backer for supportability. Their impact prompts shifts in industry principles and practices.

****3. Proficient Turn of events:**

The self-awareness that models accomplish benefits their expert turn of events. They become more flexible, versatile, and fit for taking care of many tasks, adding to their life span in the business.

****4. Mentorship and Direction:**

Models who experience self-awareness frequently take on mentorship jobs, directing hopeful models through their excursions. They share their encounters, experiences, and backing, adding to the advancement of the up and coming age of ability.

****5. Magnanimity and Social Effect:**

Models who go through self-improvement frequently utilize their foundation for generosity and social effect. They address issues like social causes, manageability, and magnanimous drives, leaving a tradition of positive change.

5.1. Adaptability and Resilience

In the always advancing and exceptionally cutthroat universe of design and demonstrating, versatility and flexibility are two characteristics that are attractive as well as fundamental for progress. Models exploring the runway and the more extensive design industry experience a progression of difficulties, including moving patterns, requesting workplaces, and extraordinary rivalry. It is their capacity to adjust to these difficulties and their flexibility even with difficulty that separates them. In this investigation of flexibility and versatility, we dig into the basic job these characteristics play in a model's excursion, looking at how they are sharpened, tried, and utilized to beat the deterrents that come their direction.

The Idea of the Demonstrating Business:

The demonstrating business is a dynamic and speedy climate, described by consistent change and elevated requirements. Models frequently wind up in testing circumstances that request speedy reasoning, the capacity to adjust, and versatility to finish what has been started.

****1. Changing Patterns and Feel:**

Design is a flighty industry, with patterns and feel continually developing. What is stylish today might be obsolete tomorrow. Models should adjust to evolving styles, encapsulate different looks, and remain important in the steadily moving scene of design.

****2. Extraordinary Rivalry:**

The opposition in the demonstrating business is furious. Models should battle with various others competing for similar open doors. This elevated degree of contest requires flexibility to stick out and versatility to endure dismissals and misfortunes.

****3. Requests of the Runway:**

Strolling the runway requires accuracy, balance, and the capacity to adjust to various architects' dreams. The tension of a live crowd and the need to execute perfect exhibitions request both versatility and strength.

****4. Various Tasks:**

Models take on a great many tasks, from design shows and photoshoots to publication work and brand crusades. These assorted jobs require flexibility to flawlessly switch between various styles and ideas.

5. Worldwide Travel:

Worldwide appointments and travel are normal in the business. Models frequently end up working in new areas and social settings, requesting flexibility and versatility to acclimate to new conditions.

6. Media and Public Investigation:

The appearance of web-based entertainment has presented models to steady open examination. Pessimistic remarks, online analysis, and the strain to keep an organized web-based picture require close to home strength and flexibility.

Sharpening Versatility:

Flexibility is an expertise that models constantly sharpen all through their vocations. It includes the capacity to conform to new circumstances, answer criticism, and embrace change as a dependable friend in the demonstrating business.

1. Remaining Refreshed on Patterns:

Models need to stay fully informed regarding the most popular trend patterns and industry improvements. This includes concentrating on style magazines, following planners and brands, and looking for motivation from different sources.

2. Working with Various Styles:

Flexibility frequently implies having the option to exemplify a different scope of styles, from high design and couture to streetwear and relaxed looks. Models should be chameleonic, changing their appearances to fit the prerequisites of a particular undertaking.

3. Adaptability in Development:

The capacity to adjust to the runway and different demonstrating tasks requires adaptability in development. Models participate in activities and preparing to keep up with their actual flexibility, which is essential for executing various postures and strolls.

4. Strength Despite Dismissals:

Dismissals are a typical event in the displaying business. The capacity to adjust and push ahead subsequent to being turned down for tasks or castings is a significant part of a model's vocation.

5. Dealing with Analysis:

Models frequently get input and analysis from photographic artists, planners, and clients. Figuring out how to adjust and develop from valuable analysis while keeping up with profound versatility is fundamental.

Testing Versatility:

Strength is the ability to endure difficulty and quickly return from difficulties. In the demonstrating business, flexibility is tried in different ways, and models figure out how to foster this quality through their encounters.

1. Dismissals and Misfortunes:

Models face various dismissals and misfortunes in their professions. It very well may be missing out on a sought after booking or being disregarded for a design show. Flexibility assists models with adapting to disillusionments and keep seeking after their objectives.

2. Analysis and Strain:

Models frequently work in high-pressure conditions, where they are supposed to faultlessly perform. They might experience requesting photographic artists or troublesome clients. Strength assists them with overseeing pressure and analysis while keeping an expert disposition.

3. Adjusting Individual and Expert Life:

The demonstrating calling can interest, with unpredictable hours and broad travel. Adjusting individual life and work is a steady test that requires profound flexibility.

4. Industry Magnificence Principles:

The strain to adjust to industry magnificence principles can sincerely burden. Strength assists models with keeping a sound self-perception and fearlessness.

5. Online Investigation:

The universe of virtual entertainment brings both praise and analysis. Models are frequently presented to online examination and negative remarks. Strength is vital to dealing with the profound effect of public input.

Procedures for Creating Strength:

Strength is a quality that can be developed and created. Models utilize different techniques to improve their flexibility and endure the tensions of the business.

****1. The capacity to understand anyone on a deeper level:**

Creating the capacity to appreciate individuals on a profound level permits models to grasp their feelings, as well as the feelings of others. It helps with overseeing pressure and connections actually.

****2. Emotional wellness and Prosperity:**

Focusing on emotional wellness and prosperity is essential. Models participate in taking care of oneself works on, including reflection, care, and stress the executives procedures.

****3. Emotionally supportive networks:**

Building solid emotionally supportive networks with companions, family, coaches, and individual models is an essential system for keeping up with profound versatility.

****4. Self-Sympathy:**

Rehearsing self-sympathy includes being benevolent to oneself, especially in snapshots of disappointment or difficulty. It is a fundamental apparatus for encouraging strength.

****5. Compromise Abilities:**

Mastering compromise abilities assists models with exploring tough spots and connections. Viable correspondence can diminish pressure and add to strength.

Utilizing Flexibility and Strength:

Flexibility and strength are not simply abilities to survive in the demonstrating business; they are resources that models can use to succeed in their professions.

****1. Adaptability:**

Flexibility permits models to be adaptable and take on a great many tasks. They can flawlessly progress starting with one style then onto the next, making them profoundly pursued by clients and architects.

2. Life span in the Business:

Models who adjust to changing patterns and stay versatile even with difficulty will generally have long and persevering through professions. Their capacity to remain significant guarantees a persistent stream of chances.

3. Impressive skill:

Versatile and strong models frequently show impressive skill in their associations with clients, architects, photographic artists, and partners. This impressive skill prompts positive working connections and rehash appointments.

4. Impact and Backing:

Models who have bridled their versatility and strength frequently become advocates for positive change in the business. They utilize their foundation to resolve issues like variety, inclusivity, supportability, and emotional wellness.

5. Mentorship and Direction:

Strong and versatile models frequently take on mentorship jobs, directing hopeful models through their excursions. They share their encounters, bits of knowledge, and backing, adding to the advancement of the up and coming age of ability.

The Getting through Excursion:

In the demonstrating business, flexibility and strength are not simply abilities; they are characteristics that models convey with them all through their professions and lives. The difficulties they face and the changes they go through are a demonstration of the getting through nature of their excursion. Demonstrating is a calling that requests something other than great looks; it requires a tireless soul and the capacity to adjust to a consistently impacting world, flourishing notwithstanding difficulty.

5.2. Self-Discovery and Self-Confidence

The excursion of a model in the realm of style and displaying isn't simply a vocation; it is a significant course of self-revelation and fearlessness building. The requests of the business, combined with the openness to different encounters and people, give a novel chance to models to investigate their characters and fabricate a significant identity assuredness. In this investigation of self-disclosure and fearlessness, we dig into the basic job these perspectives play in a model's excursion, looking at how they are developed, sharpened, and utilized to succeed in the business as well as to flourish in life past the runway.

The Mission for Self-Revelation:

The excursion of self-disclosure is in many cases the main impetus behind a hopeful model's choice to enter the business. The craving to investigate one's character, both concerning actual appearance and individual person, is a strong inspiration.

1. **Character Investigation:**

   Design and demonstrating give a material to character investigation. As models explore different avenues regarding different looks, styles, and feel, they gain a more profound comprehension of their own personality. The business energizes singularity and uniqueness, encouraging an identity disclosure.

2. **Social Responsiveness:**

   Working in the design and demonstrating industry opens models to a heap of societies, customs, and viewpoints. Global appointments require a versatility to different social settings, and this cultivates social responsiveness and expands perspectives.

3. **Certainty Building:**

   One of the most extraordinary parts of a demonstrating profession is the improvement of self-assurance. Models figure out how to convey themselves with balance, ooze self-assuredness, and task a picture of self-conviction. The certainty they gain helps their vocations as well as reaches out to their own lives.

4. **Profound Flexibility:**

The demonstrating calling is requesting, frequently requiring profound versatility despite dismissal, analysis, and the tensions of the business. Models foster the ability to return quickly from difficulties, adapt to difficulty, and keep areas of strength for an of self.

5. **Amazing skill and Versatility:**

Style and demonstrating request an elevated degree of impressive skill, dependability, and flexibility. These abilities, when sharpened in the business, are significant fundamental abilities that advantage models in different parts of their lives.

6. **Monetary Education:**

The conflicting pay examples of the demonstrating calling require monetary proficiency. Models figure out how to deal with their profit, plan for times of lower pay, and settle on shrewd monetary choices, adding to their general prosperity.

7. **Promotion and Generosity:**

The course of self-disclosure frequently drives models to promotion and magnanimity. Many models utilize their foundation to resolve issues like variety, inclusivity, supportability, and social causes. They look to have a beneficial outcome past their demonstrating professions.

Changing Through Encounters:

Models go through significant changes through the encounters they aggregate in the business. The unique idea of the calling, with its high-pressure conditions and various tasks, shapes their own and proficient development.

1. **Imaginative Investigation:**

Working with different originators, photographic artists, and beauticians permits models to submerge themselves in innovative strategies. They explore different avenues regarding different styles and feel, frequently pushing the limits of their usual ranges of familiarity. This innovative investigation impacts their demonstrating professions as well as their own style and creative interests.

2. **Worldwide Openness:**
Worldwide appointments open models to a heap of societies, dialects, and customs. The capacity to adjust to various conditions and interface with people from different foundations enhances their own lives and expands their perspectives.

3. **Style and Industry Experiences:**
Models are at the bleeding edge of style and industry experiences. They gain an inside and out comprehension of the design world, which frequently impacts their own style and design decisions.

4. **Systems administration and Relationship Building:**
Building associations with industry experts, from originators and photographic artists to cosmetics craftsmen and beauticians, upgrades a model's social and expert organization. These connections frequently lead to amazing open doors and coordinated efforts past their demonstrating vocations.

5. **The ability to understand people at their core:**
The inner difficulties of the business expect models to foster capacity to appreciate people on a deeper level. They become more sensitive to their own feelings and the feelings of others, cultivating better connections in their own lives.

6. **Versatility and Flexibility:**

Versatility is sharpened through persevering and adjusting to difficulties. The capacity to quickly return from dismissals and adjust to changing conditions furnishes models with fundamental abilities.

Adjusting Individual and Expert Development:
Offsetting self-awareness with the requests of a demonstrating vocation is a basic part of a model's excursion. The capacity to explore the double liabilities of a high-profile calling and individual prosperity is a demonstration of a model's development and development.

1. **Balance between serious and fun activities:**
   Keeping a balance between serious and fun activities can be trying for models, particularly when they need to travel regularly and work unpredictable hours. The capacity to focus on private prosperity, connections, and taking care of oneself exhibits self-awareness.

2. **Connections and Family:**
   Models frequently need to oversee connections and family responsibilities close by their vocations. The advancement of sound connections and close to home bonds with friends and family is a fundamental part of self-awareness.

3. **Taking care of oneself and Wellbeing:**
   Models focus on taking care of oneself and health to support their professions and individual lives. This incorporates actual wellness, psychological well-being practices, skincare, and unwinding strategies.

4. **Learning and Improvement:**
   Models proceed to master and foster their abilities all through their professions. They take part in studios, courses, and personal growth drives, mirroring their obligation to self-awareness.

5. **Monetary Obligation:**

Exploring the demonstrating business' conflicting pay designs requires monetary obligation. The capacity to oversee funds, plan for the future, and go with informed choices adds to by and large prosperity.

The Enduring Effect:
The self-awareness and self-revelation that models experience have an enduring effect that reaches out past their professions. These changes shape their lives, connections, and the heritage they leave in the business.

1. **Validness and Strengthening:**
   Models who go through self-improvement frequently become

advocates for realness and strengthening. They utilize their foundation to urge others to embrace their distinction, put stock in themselves, and have a beneficial outcome.

2. **Effect on Industry Practices:**
Models who advocate for positive change frequently impact industry rehearses. They challenge obsolete excellence standards, advance variety and inclusivity, and backer for supportability. Their impact prompts shifts in industry principles and practices.

3. **Proficient Turn of events:**
The self-improvement that models accomplish benefits their expert turn of events. They become more flexible, versatile, and equipped for taking care of a great many tasks, adding to their life span in the business.

4. **Mentorship and Direction:**
Models who experience self-improvement frequently take on mentorship jobs, directing hopeful models through their excursions. They share their encounters, experiences, and backing, adding to the improvement of the up and coming age of ability.

5. **Generosity and Social Effect:**

Models who go through self-awareness frequently utilize their foundation for magnanimity and social effect. They address issues like social causes, manageability, and generous drives, leaving a tradition of positive change.

5.3. The Transition from Aspiring to Professional

The excursion from a hopeful model to an expert in the realm of style and demonstrating is an extraordinary and testing process. It addresses the climax of difficult work, devotion, and a constant quest for one's fantasies. Hopeful models set out on this excursion bearing in mind the end goal of coming to the top, yet the way is full of deterrents, rivalry, and the need to substantiate oneself ceaselessly. In this investigation of the progress from seeking to proficient, we dig into the basic stages, encounters, and attitude moves that describe this excursion and the variables that different the people who cause it from the individuals who to don't.

The Hopeful Model's Fantasy:

The excursion starts with a fantasy — a fantasy about strolling the runway, gracing magazine covers, and being the substance of top brands. Hopeful models frequently venerate laid out figures in the business and long to emulate their example. This fantasy is the flash that touches off the fire of desire and moves them into the universe of displaying.

****1. Motivation and Good examples:**

Hopeful models draw motivation from industry legends and good examples. They intently follow the vocations of eminent models, fashioners, and photographic artists, expecting to imitate their prosperity.

****2. The Enthusiasm for Design:**

A certifiable enthusiasm for design and innovativeness frequently supports the desires of models. The charm of extraordinary plans, creative articulations, and the possibility of being a piece of the style world drives their fantasies.

****3. The Craving for Acknowledgment:**

The goal for acknowledgment is a typical inspiration. Models long for the approval and popularity that accompany being an expert in the business.

****4. Self-improvement and Self-Disclosure:**

The excursion from trying to proficient addresses a critical period of self-awareness and self-disclosure. Hopeful models utilize the business as a stage to investigate their personalities, construct fearlessness, and foster flexibility.

The Beginning stages:

Hopeful models enter the business with a feeling of marvel and desire, yet they should explore the underlying stages set apart by tryouts, castings, and dismissals.

****1. Organization Tryouts:**

Hopeful models go to organization tryouts, where they present their portfolios and stroll for headhunters. These tryouts frequently bring about dismissals, as the business is profoundly serious, and a couple of get it done.

2. Ability and Advancement Organizations:

A few hopeful models sign with ability and improvement offices that give direction, preparing, and valuable open doors for openness. These organizations assume a vital part in supporting arising ability.

3. Portfolio Building:

Hopeful models work on building areas of strength for a with the assistance of picture takers, cosmetics craftsmen, and beauticians. A convincing portfolio is their reason for living card in the business.

4. Organizing:

Organizing is an indispensable part of the beginning stages. Models go to industry occasions, style shows, and interface with picture takers and architects to lay out connections that might prompt future open doors.

5. Dismissals and Dissatisfactions:

The beginning stages are frequently set apart by dismissals and dissatisfactions. Hopeful models should foster strength to adapt to these misfortunes and keep up with their assurance.

The Change Stages:

The change from trying to proficient is set apart by huge achievements that set up for a maintainable vocation in displaying.

1. First Appointments:

A vital second in a model's change is their most memorable expert booking. It could be a design show, a magazine publication, or a brand crusade. This advancement approves their endeavors and makes way for additional potential open doors.

2. Office Portrayal:

Protecting portrayal with trustworthy demonstrating organizations is a huge step. Organizations furnish models with admittance to a more extensive scope of chances and the direction of experienced experts.

3. Acknowledgment and Openness:

Models start to earn respect and openness through their work. Their pictures show up in magazines, on boards, and in notices, adding to their developing profile in the business.

**4. Global Tasks:

Models who try to worldwide vocations frequently take on global tasks. Heading out abroad to work with eminent architects and picture takers expands their perspectives and opens them to various style markets.

**5. Proficient Connections:

Building solid expert associations with originators, picture takers, and clients is critical to a model's prosperity. Models who are solid, simple to work with, and keep up with positive working connections are bound to get rehash appointments.

The Outlook Shift:

The change to an expert model frequently includes a huge change in outlook. Hopeful models should develop from a condition of desire and goal to one of incredible skill, responsibility, and supportability.

**1. Incredible skill and Dependability:

Proficient models focus on reliability, readiness, and amazing skill. They comprehend that their standing is pivotal in getting rehash appointments.

**2. Nonstop Learning:

The advancing never stops for proficient models. They go to studios, classes, and get criticism to further develop their abilities consistently.

**3. Industry Mindfulness:

Proficient models stay informed about industry patterns, fashioners, and brands. They comprehend the developing scene and adjust as needs be.

**4. Individual Marking:

Models foster their own image, which includes their remarkable style, values, and picture. A solid individual brand separates them in a packed field.

**5. Mentorship and Direction:

Looking for mentorship and direction from industry veterans is normal. Proficient models gain from the people who have strolled the way before them, acquiring significant bits of knowledge and counsel.

Supporting a Profession:

Supporting a displaying vocation includes a mix of elements, from flexibility and versatility to incredible skill and a solid hard working attitude.

****1. Adaptability:**

Proficient models are flexible and can adjust to different styles, subjects, and looks. Their capacity to exemplify various characters and style makes them exceptionally pursued.

****2. Importance and Flexibility:**

Remaining applicable and versatile is urgent. Models who stay aware of the most recent patterns and stay open to change are bound to have long and prosperous vocations.

****3. Life span in the Business:**

Proficient models frequently appreciate long and getting through professions, as their capacity to keep major areas of strength for an in the business prompts a persistent stream of chances.

****4. Proficient Connections:**

Models who keep up with positive expert associations with planners, photographic artists, and clients keep on getting appointments. The business depends intensely on verbal exchange suggestions.

****5. Support and Social Effect:**

Proficient models frequently utilize their foundation for support and social effect. They address issues like variety, inclusivity, manageability, and psychological well-being, utilizing their leverage for positive change.

The Change to Fame:

For a chosen handful, the progress from trying to proficient prompts fame. Supermodels like Naomi Campbell, Kate Greenery, and Gisele Bündchen address the apex of outcome in the demonstrating scene.

****1. Notable Minutes:**

Supermodels frequently have notable minutes in their vocations, like showing up on the front of esteemed magazines, strolling for eminent planners, and turning into the essences of significant brands.

2. Worldwide Acknowledgment:

They accomplish worldwide acknowledgment and rise above the universe of style. Their names become inseparable from style, and they gain a degree of distinction that reaches out past the business.

3. Impact and Promotion:

Supermodels utilize their status to advocate for purposes they are energetic about. They become forces to be reckoned with, in style, however in the public eye all in all.

4. Heritage:

The change to fame permits models to leave an enduring heritage. They impact industry rehearses, challenge excellence standards, and motivate the up and coming age of ability.

Chapter Six

Real World Integration

The universe of style and displaying, while frequently glamorized, exists inside a more extensive setting - this present reality. As models climb in their vocations, they progressively wind up entwining with the intricacies of day to day existence. This genuine incorporation envelops a huge number of perspectives, from connections and monetary administration to cultural effect and the obligations that accompany distinction. In this investigation of genuine combination, we dive into the many-sided manners by which models explore the convergence of their demonstrating professions with the requests, difficulties, and chances of the world past the runway.

Adjusting Individual and Expert Life:

Offsetting individual existence with a thriving demonstrating profession can be a difficult accomplishment. As models rise in the business, they should arrange the double liabilities of a high-profile calling and individual prosperity.

****1. Balance between serious and fun activities:**

Keeping a balance between fun and serious activities is many times a fragile shuffling represent models. They work sporadic hours, travel often, and should set aside opportunity for taking care of oneself and individual connections.

2. Connections and Family:

Models as often as possible need to oversee connections and family responsibilities close by their vocations. The advancement of sound connections and profound bonds with friends and family is a fundamental part of genuine mix.

3. Nurturing:

Many models become guardians while effectively chasing after their professions. The obligations of life as a parent, including childcare, using time effectively, and offering close to home help, require a cautious equilibrium.

4. Taking care of oneself and Health:

Focusing on taking care of oneself and health is essential to supporting a demonstrating vocation and individual prosperity. This incorporates actual wellness, emotional well-being practices, skincare, and unwinding methods.

5. Learning and Improvement:

Models proceed to acquire and foster their abilities all through their vocations. They take part in studios, courses, and personal development drives, mirroring their obligation to self-improvement.

Monetary Administration:

The demonstrating calling's conflicting pay designs request monetary obligation and proficiency. Overseeing profit, anticipating times of lower pay, and settling on insightful monetary choices are essential to a model's prosperity.

1. Monetary Preparation:

Models should anticipate the future, taking into account their ongoing profit as well as their post-displaying profession. Effective money management, saving, and monetary arranging are essential parts of certifiable reconciliation.

2. Revenue Sources:

Expanding revenue streams is normal among models. They might participate in different tasks, from supports and brand associations to form lines and pioneering adventures, to get monetary soundness.

3. Duties and Legalities:

Exploring charge regulations and lawful commitments is a basic part of true joining. Models frequently require monetary consultants and lawful direction to guarantee consistence and ideal monetary administration.

4. Planning:

Making and sticking to spending plans is fundamental, especially during times of sporadic pay. Models should offset their costs with their profit to stay away from monetary flimsiness.

Social Effect and Support:

As models ascend in their vocations, they perceive the persuasive stages they have and their capacity to have a beneficial outcome on society. Many decide to involve their perceivability for backing and social effect.

1. Resolving Social Issues:

Models frequently become advocates for social issues like variety, inclusivity, supportability, and psychological well-being. They utilize their leverage to bring issues to light, support causes, and drive positive change.

2. Altruism:

Many models participate in altruistic undertakings, supporting beneficent associations and drives that line up with their qualities and needs. They influence their assets and status to add to significant causes.

3. Natural Manageability:

The style business is progressively centered around supportability, and models assume a part in advancing eco-accommodating practices. They advocate for manageable design decisions, dependable utilization, and harmless to the ecosystem drives.

4. Emotional well-being Mindfulness:

The requesting idea of the demonstrating business frequently requires backing for emotional well-being mindfulness. Models share their own encounters, bring issues to light, and advance the significance of taking care of oneself.

Impact and Obligation:

With expanding notoriety and acknowledgment, models bear an uplifted degree of impact and obligation. They should explore their jobs as well known individuals, figuring out the effect of their activities and decisions on their crowd.

****1. Good examples:**

Models frequently become good examples to hopeful ability and the more extensive public. They set models concerning amazing skill, morals, and fearlessness, rousing others to seek after their fantasies.

****2. Web-based Entertainment Effect:**

In the computerized age, models have a huge presence via web-based entertainment. They should utilize these stages capably, as their posts and messages contact a wide and various crowd.

****3. Picture and Portrayal:**

Models impact the manner in which society sees magnificence, style, and individual articulation. They convey the obligation of testing magnificence standards and advancing variety and inclusivity in the business.

****4. Moral Decisions:**

Models settle on moral decisions in regards to the brands they underwrite, the causes they support, and the qualities they maintain. Their choices lastingly affect their standing and social impact.

Amazing skill and Morals:

Keeping up with amazing skill and moral direct is vital for models as they explore their vocations. Their activities and choices have sweeping outcomes, and they should maintain exclusive expectations.

****1. Hard working attitude:**

Proficient models focus on dependability, readiness, and impressive skill in their work. They comprehend that their standing is significant in getting rehash appointments.

2. Uprightness:

Moral uprightness is a non-debatable part of a model's vocation. Maintaining standards like genuineness, reasonableness, and obligation is fundamental to their standing and long haul achievement.

3. Sound Rivalry:

The demonstrating business is serious, yet models should keep up with solid contest. Staying away from pernicious strategies and embracing a feeling of kinship with individual models is fundamental for an amicable workplace.

4. Support for Fair Practices:

Models frequently advocate for fair industry works on, including evenhanded compensation, different projecting, and a strong workplace. They utilize their foundation to resolve issues connected with abuse and segregation.

Influence on Industry Practices:

Proficient models frequently impact industry works on, testing obsolete guidelines and empowering positive changes.

1. Variety and Inclusivity:

Models advocate for variety and inclusivity in projecting, advancing models of different foundations, body types, and sexes. Their endeavors lead to a more delegate and comprehensive industry.

2. Supportability:

The design business' supportability endeavors are fundamentally molded by models who champion eco-accommodating style decisions, moral obtaining, and mindful creation.

3. Psychological wellness Backing:

Models have been instrumental in upholding for emotional wellness support inside the business. They feature the requirement for close to home prosperity and the significance of emotionally supportive networks.

****4. Engaging Others:**

Proficient models frequently utilize their situations to engage hopeful ability and give direction. They become endlessly coaches, supporting the up and coming age of models.

Keeping a Long and Getting through Vocation:

Proficient models frequently appreciate long and getting through professions. Supporting a displaying vocation includes a mix of variables, from flexibility and versatility to impressive skill and a solid hard working attitude.

****1. Adaptability:**

Proficient models are flexible and can adjust to different styles, subjects, and looks. Their capacity to epitomize various characters and style makes them exceptionally pursued.

****2. Significance and Versatility:**

Remaining pertinent and versatile is vital. Models who stay aware of the most recent patterns and stay open to change are bound to have long and prosperous professions.

****3. Life span in the Business:**

Proficient models frequently appreciate long and getting through professions, as their capacity to keep areas of strength for an in the business prompts a consistent stream of chances.

****4. Proficient Connections:**

Models who keep up with positive expert associations with originators, photographic artists, and clients keep on getting appointments. The business depends intensely on informal exchange suggestions.

****5. Support and Social Effect:**

Proficient models frequently utilize their foundation for support and social effect. They address issues like variety, inclusivity, manageability, and psychological wellness, capitalizing on their leverage for positive change.

Embracing This present reality:

As models incorporate with this present reality, they should embrace the multi-layered nature of their professions and lives. This incorporation includes a powerful interchange of individual, proficient, and cultural components.

1. Realness:

Embracing this present reality requires genuineness. Models should stay consistent with their qualities and convictions, even despite industry pressures.

2. Adjusted Needs:

Adjusting individual life, profession, and cultural obligations requires clear needs. Models should figure out what makes the biggest difference to them and adjust their decisions likewise.

3. Obligation:

With extraordinary impact comes incredible obligation. Models bear the obligation of being positive good examples and promoters for change.

4. Adaptability and Variation:

Embracing this present reality includes adaptability and variation to evolving conditions. Models should stay open to new open doors and difficulties.

6.1. Preparing Models for Life Beyond the Runway

The demonstrating business offers hopeful people the commitment of marvelousness, acknowledgment, and an intriguing profession. In any case, similar to any calling, a displaying profession at last reaches a conclusion. Getting ready models for life past the runway is a fundamental and frequently disregarded part of the business. Models, no matter what their degree of progress, should explore the change to post-demonstrating life. This cycle includes self-improvement, schooling, monetary preparation, and the development of abilities and organizations that will empower them to prevail in a world that exists a long ways past the spotlight. In this investigation, we dive into the different parts of planning models for life past the runway, underlining the significance of a comprehensive way to deal with this change.

The Limited Idea of Displaying:

The universe of displaying is prestigious for its excitement and fabulousness, yet it is essential to comprehend that it is a transient profession. The limited idea of displaying vocations requires proactive groundwork for life past the runway.

1. Age and Market Requests:

Demonstrating is an industry where age assumes a critical part. As models become older, the interest for their administrations frequently diminishes, especially in the high style industry. This reality expects models to plan for changes on the lookout.

2. Market Patterns and Inclinations:

Market patterns and inclinations shift with time. What is thought of "in" or "in vogue" today might change from here on out. Models should expect and adjust to these patterns.

3. Individual Decisions:

Models might decide to resign from the business anytime for individual or expert reasons. Whether it's to zero in on family, investigate other vocation ways, or seek after additional schooling, making arrangements for life past the runway is fundamental.

All encompassing Planning:

Getting ready for life past the runway includes a diverse methodology that tends to different parts of a model's life and vocation.

1. Self-awareness:

Models should take part in self-awareness to assemble fearlessness, the ability to understand anyone at their core, and strength. These characteristics are significant for life past the runway.

2. Instruction and Ability Improvement:

Acquiring information and creating abilities are basic for post-demonstrating vocations. Models ought to investigate instructive open doors, professional preparation, and individual interests.

3. Monetary Preparation:

Monetary arranging is fundamental to guarantee a steady and secure future. Models need to spending plan, save, contribute, and go with informed monetary choices.

4. Building Proficient Organizations:

Models can use their current expert organizations to investigate new profession open doors. Associations with photographic artists, creators, and industry experts can open entryways in different fields.

5. Mentorship and Direction:

Looking for mentorship and direction from experienced models who have effectively changed to different vocations is priceless. They can give bits of knowledge and backing.

Self-improvement for Strength:

Strength is a basic quality that models should develop, as it sets them up to adjust to the inescapable changes and difficulties that accompany life past the runway.

1. Building Fearlessness:

Certainty is a vital part of flexibility. Models can take part in fearlessness building works out, self-reflection, and self-confirmation rehearses.

2. The ability to understand anyone on a profound level:

Models should foster ability to understand anyone on a profound level to explore the intricacies of life past the runway. This includes understanding and dealing with feelings, as well as relating to other people.

3. Survival techniques:

Models need to foster compelling survival techniques to oversee pressure and misfortune. Care, unwinding methods, and stress the executives abilities are valuable.

4. Individual Personality:

Self-personality is frequently intently attached to a demonstrating vocation. Models ought to deal with building a self-appreciation that rises above their calling, embracing different parts of their character.

5. Keeping up with Emotional well-being:

Focusing on emotional wellness through treatment, advising, or support bunches is fundamental. A solid underpinning of mental prosperity prepares models for the difficulties they might look from now on.

Schooling and Ability Improvement:

Training and ability improvement give models the apparatuses they need to change into new professions or fields of interest.

1. Proceeding with Training:

Models can seek after additional training in fields, for example, business, style plan, correspondences, or any region that lines up with their inclinations and objectives.

2. Professional Preparation:

Procuring commonsense abilities through professional preparation or courses can prompt open doors in fields like excellence, cosmetics creativity, styling, or photography.

3. Pioneering Tries:

Models with a pioneering soul can investigate business valuable open doors, for example, beginning their own style brands, cosmetics lines, or demonstrating offices.

4. Purposeful ventures:

Models can commit time to meaningful ventures, which might prompt open doors in imaginative businesses like craftsmanship, music, or composing.

5. Adaptable Abilities:

Models ought to distinguish and level up adaptable abilities from their demonstrating vocations, like correspondence, flexibility, and systems administration.

Monetary Preparation and Steadiness:

Monetary arranging is fundamental to give models monetary steadiness and security for their post-demonstrating life.

1. Planning and Saving:

Models should make spending plans and save a part of their pay for future monetary security. This incorporates making arrangements for times of lower pay and retirement.

2. Speculation Systems:

Finding out about various speculation potential open doors, like stocks, land, or retirement accounts, means quite a bit to get monetary development.

3. Home Preparation:

Making an exhaustive bequest plan, including wills, trusts, and recipients, guarantees that resources are disseminated by a model's desires.

4. Monetary Consultants:

Models can look for guidance from monetary experts to arrive at informed conclusions about their funds and ventures.

5. Numerous Revenue Sources:

Enhancing revenue streams through speculations, side organizations, or extra vocations can give monetary security.

Building Proficient Organizations:

Utilizing existing proficient organizations is a significant asset for models looking for valuable open doors in various businesses.

1. Industry Connections:

Keeping up with associations with photographic artists, planners, cosmetics craftsmen, beauticians, and other industry experts can prompt vocation potential open doors past displaying.

2. Cooperative Ventures:

Teaming up on tasks or adventures with contacts from the business can prompt creative open doors.

3. Organizing Occasions:

Going to systems administration occasions, meetings, and workshops in related fields opens models to new associations and possibilities.

4. Proficient Associations:

Joining proficient associations connected with areas of interest or ability can prompt significant systems administration valuable open doors.

5. Online Presence:

Using on the web stages, including virtual entertainment and expert sites, can assist models with extending their organizations and feature their abilities.

Mentorship and Direction:

Looking for mentorship and direction from experienced models who have effectively progressed to new professions is an important asset.

1. Tutor Mentee Connections:

Laying out tutor mentee connections permits models to acquire bits of knowledge, counsel, and direction from the individuals who have strolled the way before them.

2. Profession Arranging:

Tutors can help models in fostering a lifelong arrangement, recognizing potential profession ways, and putting forth reasonable objectives.

3. Defeating Difficulties:

Guides offer important help in defeating difficulties and snags during the progress cycle.

4. Proficient Turn of events:

Coaches frequently guide models in their expert turn of events, including ability building and self-improvement.

5. Motivation and Inspiration:

Guides move and spur models to investigate additional opportunities and stay focused on their yearnings.

Genuine Examples of overcoming adversity:

Genuine examples of overcoming adversity of models who have effectively changed to different vocations act as motivations for those exploring the post-displaying stage.

1. Business venture:

A few models have wandered into business venture by beginning their design lines, magnificence brands, or displaying offices.

2. Media and Amusement:

Models have made progress in the media and media outlet, seeking after vocations in acting, facilitating, or reporting.

3. Style Plan:

Models enthusiastically for configuration have become fruitful style fashioners, making their lines or teaming up with laid out brands.

4. Promotion and Altruism:

Many models utilize their notoriety and impact to become advocates for social causes and altruistic drives.

5. Training and The scholarly community:

A models progress to vocations in schooling and the scholarly world, becoming style educators, tutors, or industry specialists.

Adjusting Current Profession and Future Goals:

Offsetting a displaying profession with arrangements for life past the runway requires cautious preparation and association.

****1. Using time productively:**

Powerful using time productively is fundamental for shuffle demonstrating responsibilities, self-improvement, and schooling or expertise building exercises.

****2. Laying out Boundaries:**

Models ought to decide their needs, perceiving what means a lot to them in the short and long haul.

****3. Adaptable Profession Decisions:**

Models ought to pick professions or instructive ways that offer adaptability to oblige their demonstrating plans.

****4. Emotionally supportive networks:**

Having areas of strength for a framework, including companions, family, coaches, and specialists, can make the change smoother.

****5. Clear Objectives:**

Laying out clear objectives for post-demonstrating vocations assists models with remaining fixed on their goals.

6.2. Post-Show Opportunities and Challenges

The fabulousness and charm of the design world frequently get everyone's attention, except the post-show stage is a urgent part in a model's excursion. Subsequent to swaggering the runway and charming crowds, models experience a perplexing exhibit of chances and difficulties that shape their fates. These encounters reach out a long ways past the catwalk, including all that from professional success and expert connections to self-improvement and transformation to the consistently developing design industry. In this investigation of post-show open doors and difficulties, we dig into the multi-layered parts of a model's life once the runway lights have diminished.

Post-Show Potential open doors:

The outcome of a style show brings an abundance of chances for models hoping to expand on their runway achievement. These amazing open doors frequently act as venturing stones to additional acknowledgment and professional success.

1. Design Missions and Articles:

Models who intrigue on the runway frequently get the attention of creators and photographic artists, prompting amazing open doors for style missions and publication highlights. These undertakings offer openness and pay.

2. Business and Brand Supports:

Models oftentimes secure business agreements and brand supports after fruitful runway appearances. These organizations can turn out rewarding revenue and expanded perceivability.

3. Runway Reverberation:

A solid runway presence can prompt recurrent solicitations for future design shows, cementing a model's status inside the business.

4. Worldwide Acknowledgment:

Worldwide runway appearances can open ways to worldwide acknowledgment, permitting models to work in different style capitals all over the planet.

5. Industry Systems administration:

Style shows furnish models with unrivaled systems administration amazing open doors. They can lay out associations with planners, specialists, and other industry experts, which can prompt future coordinated efforts.

6. Professional success:

Generally welcomed runway exhibitions frequently move models to more elevated levels inside the business, like couture and high fashion shows.

Proficient Connections:

Supporting proficient connections is a foundation of progress in the displaying scene. After a style show, models have the chance to fortify associations with industry experts.

1. Fashioners:

An effective joint effort with a fashioner can prompt recurrent appointments and organizations for future shows and missions.

2. Photographic artists:

Photographic artists frequently search out models who have had an enduring effect on the runway. These picture takers might work with models on article shoots, promoting efforts, or different ventures.

3. Beauticians and Cosmetics Craftsmen:

Building associations with beauticians and cosmetics craftsmen can prompt cooperative open doors later on, as these experts regularly assume a urgent part in design missions and publications.

4. Displaying Offices:

Displaying organizations might perceive the capability of models who perform well in style shows and proposition them extra open doors and portrayal.

5. Industry Insiders:

Supporting associations with industry insiders, for example, projecting chiefs and show makers can prompt further runway appointments and acquaintances with compelling figures in the style world.

Growing Portfolio:

Partaking in design shows gives models the amazing chance to enhance and extend their portfolios, exhibiting their flexibility and reach.

1. Exhibiting Adaptability:

Models who succeed on the runway can show their capacity to epitomize different looks and styles, making them more interesting to creators and clients for a large number of undertakings.

2. Investigating Themed Shows:

Themed design shows frequently urge models to investigate various characters and style, adding profundity to their portfolios.

3. Featuring Mark Walk:

Style shows permit models to grandstand their unmistakable runway walk, which can turn into a particular piece of their image and appeal to fashioners.

****4. Adjusting to Various Styles:**

Partaking in assorted design shows empowers models to adjust to various styles, feel, and creative dreams, improving their attractiveness.

****5. Building a Conspicuous Presence:**

A solid presence on the runway adds to a model's acknowledgment inside the business, which can prompt different open doors.

Cultural and Social Effect:

The impact of design shows stretches out past the business, affecting society and culture in critical ways.

****1. Starting Precedents:**

Style shows frequently set precedents for the impending season, affecting the selections of planners, purchasers, and retailers.

****2. Social Portrayal:**

Models who take part in runway shows can possibly address their way of life or character, adding to expanded variety and inclusivity inside the design world.

****3. Advancing Qualities:**

Design shows can advance qualities like supportability, body energy, and emotional wellness mindfulness, giving models a stage to advocate for significant causes.

****4. Motivational Figures:**

Models who succeed on the runway can become motivational figures for trying ability, empowering them to seek after their fantasies and break limits inside the business.

****5. Honorary pathway Appearances:**

A fruitful runway vocation can prompt honorary pathway solicitations and appearances at high-profile occasions, further lifting a model's public profile.

Challenges in the Post-Show Stage:

While post-show open doors are bountiful, models should likewise explore provokes interesting to this period of their professions. These difficulties can go from industry tensions to individual changes.

****1. Furious Contest:**

The displaying business is exceptionally aggressive, and models should keep on showing off their abilities in an industry where patterns and inclinations regularly change.

**2. Market Immersion:

The market can become soaked with models, making it fundamental for models to stick out and constantly adjust to stay important.

**3. Conflicting Pay:

Models frequently experience conflicting pay designs, with variances among pinnacle and lean periods.

**4. Age and Market Requests:

Models should think about the effect old enough on their profession. The interest for more seasoned models in high design is in many cases restricted, provoking the requirement for broadening.

**5. Industry Tensions:

Models might experience industry pressures connected with self-perception, appearance, and magnificence principles, requiring versatility and fearlessness.

**6. Burnout:

The requesting idea of the business can prompt physical and close to home burnout. Models should focus on taking care of oneself to forestall burnout.

**7. Emotional well-being:

Models can confront huge pressure, dismissal, and investigation, requiring an emphasis on psychological well-being and close to home prosperity.

**8. Personality Shift:

Progressing from a displaying character to a post-demonstrating personality can be testing, expecting models to rethink their self-idea.

**9. Life span and Manageability:

Keeping a long and getting through profession in demonstrating frequently requires versatility and supportability in a quickly evolving industry.

**10. Moral Contemplations:

Models might have to explore moral contemplations, for example, supporting brands or items that line up with their qualities.

11. Monetary Preparation:

Overseeing funds during times of conflicting pay and making arrangements for the future are basic parts of a model's profession.

Self-improvement and Transformation:

Models should participate in self-improvement and transformation to explore the intricacies of the post-show stage.

1. Self-Revelation:

Models frequently go through self-revelation to grasp their qualities, interests, and desires past the runway.

2. Schooling and Expertise Building:

Proceeded with schooling and ability building are fundamental for models to investigate new vocation ways or areas of premium.

3. Flexibility:

Flexibility to new open doors and difficulties is essential for models to flourish in the always developing design industry.

4. Close to home Strength:

Developing close to home strength is fundamental to explore industry tensions and individual difficulties.

5. Character Past Demonstrating:

Models ought to chip away at fostering a personality that rises above their displaying vocation, embracing different parts of their life and interests.

Proficient Connections and Backing:

Keeping up with and utilizing proficient connections and emotionally supportive networks is basic to a model's progress in the post-show stage.

1. Organizing:

Proceeding to coordinate with industry experts, guides, and individual models is indispensable for getting to potential open doors and backing.

2. Mentorship:

Looking for mentorship and direction from experienced models and industry specialists can give important bits of knowledge and course.

****3. Mental and Consistent encouragement:**

Models might need mental and profound help to adapt to industry tensions and individual difficulties.

****4. Monetary Direction:**

Looking for guidance from monetary experts can assist models with settling on informed conclusions about their funds and speculations.

****5. Proficient Turn of events:**

Continuous expert improvement is essential for models to stay serious and versatile.

Genuine Examples of overcoming adversity:

Genuine examples of overcoming adversity of models who have explored the post-show stage and made enduring progress act as motivations for those emulating their example.

****1. Business:**

Models who have effectively changed to business venture by beginning their style lines, beauty care products brands, or displaying offices.

****2. Media and Diversion:**

Models who have made progress in the media and media outlet, chasing after vocations in acting, facilitating, or reporting.

****3. Style Plan:**

Models enthusiastically for plan who have become fruitful style creators, making their lines or working together with laid out brands.

****4. Support and Charity:**

Many models utilize their distinction and impact to become advocates for social causes and altruistic drives.

6.3. Balancing Fame and Reality

Popularity has an enchanting charm. It illustrates a daily existence loaded up with charm, acknowledgment, and achievement. In the demonstrating scene, accomplishing popularity is in many cases one of a definitive yearnings. The charm of distinction isn't restricted to models; it's a worldwide peculiarity in the time of virtual entertainment, unscripted television, and immediate superstar. Notwithstanding, behind the splendid lights and revering fans lies a complex and frequently testing reality. Adjusting popularity and the truth is a point that rises above the demonstrating business and dives into the major parts of human brain science, cultural elements, and the quest for joy. In this investigation, we take apart the polarity of acclaim, examining its commitments, challenges, and the effect it has on people and society at large.

The Appeal of Notoriety:

Popularity has been an immortal goal for some, determined by a craving for acknowledgment, impact, and the satisfaction of cultural assumptions.

****1. Acknowledgment and Approval:**

Distinction frequently likens to public acknowledgment, an affirmation that one has accomplished a specific degree of importance or achievement.

****2. Impact and Effect:**

Popularity accompanies the ability to impact others, whether in molding feelings, pushing for purposes, or starting precedents.

****3. Monetary Prizes:**

Popular people frequently appreciate worthwhile open doors in diversion, supports, and coordinated efforts that lead to monetary prizes.

****4. Lavish Way of life:**

Carrying on with a lavish way of life, complete with planner closets, colorful excursions, and rich homes, is a typical charm of popularity.

****5. Loving Fans and Societal position:**

Notoriety frequently brings loving fans, economic wellbeing, and the feeling of being essential for a selective and favored circle.

The Model's Point of view:

In the demonstrating scene, popularity holds a one of a kind allure. Models are at the front of design, with the possibility to become easily recognized names. This appeal brings people into the business, energized by fantasies about strolling the world's most lofty runways and gracing the fronts of top magazines.

1. High Design Fame:

For some models, the possibility of accomplishing high design fame is an attractive power. They imagine themselves as the following supermodel, ruling the runway and catching the world's consideration.

2. Worldwide Acknowledgment:

The runway gives a stage to worldwide acknowledgment. Models can become symbols, addressing the encapsulation of excellence and style.

3. Monetary Prizes:

Acclaim in the displaying scene frequently means significant profit, with top models ordering huge charges for their administrations.

4. Social Impact:

Models who accomplish popularity can become social powerhouses, forming excellence goals, style, and cultural principles.

5. The VIP Way of life:

Distinction in the demonstrating business is firmly connected with the big name way of life, with admittance to elite occasions, top of the line design, and a sample of extravagance.

Difficulties of Distinction:

Behind the sparkling façade of distinction lie significant difficulties that can influence both the individual and society in general.

1. Loss of Security:

Popularity frequently comes to the detriment of individual security. The consistent examination by the media and general society can intrusive and trouble.

2. Mental and Close to home Cost:

The strain to keep a public picture and measure up to cultural assumptions can prompt mental and close to home strain. Models are not safe to the mental cost of popularity.

3. Disengagement:

Strangely, popularity can confine. High-profile people might find it challenging to shape valid associations, prompting depression and a feeling of separation.

4. Unreasonable Assumptions:

The assumptions that go with notoriety are much of the time ridiculous and impossible, prompting pressure and tension.

5. Public Examination:

Each part of a celebrity's life, from their appearance to their activities, is dependent upon public examination, which can genuinely deplete.

The Model's Battle:

Models who accomplish distinction face these difficulties close by industry-explicit tensions.

1. Self-perception and Psychological wellness:

Models, specifically, wrestle with self-perception issues and psychological wellness challenges because of the business' accentuation on appearance and actual norms.

2. Balance between fun and serious activities:

Adjusting notoriety and the requests of a demonstrating vocation can challenge. Models frequently need to make penances in their own lives to meet their expert commitments.

3. Adapting to Dismissal:

In the demonstrating scene, dismissal is a steady friend, in any event, for renowned models. Adapting to dismissal and keeping up with confidence is an unending battle.

4. Industry Tensions:

Models who accomplish distinction are feeling the squeeze to stay at the center of attention, stick to industry principles, and live up to the assumptions of fashioners and clients.

5. Cultural Impact:

Notoriety in the demonstrating scene can add to cultural excellence beliefs and norms, affecting how people see themselves and their self-esteem.

The Clouded Side of Notoriety:

Notoriety can have a clouded side, with accounts of people who have been consumed by its charm and confronted terrible results.

1. Substance Misuse:

The tensions of distinction frequently lead to substance maltreatment as people look for comfort or departure from the serious public look.

2. Emotional wellness Battles:

Emotional wellness battles, including sadness and nervousness, are predominant among popular people who wrestle with the mental cost of distinction.

3. Embarrassments and Contentions:

Distinction can bring reputation too. Embarrassments and discussions frequently become media grub, discoloring notorieties and causing trouble.

4. Relationship Strain:

Acclaim can strain connections, as accomplices, companions, and relatives wrestle with the progressions in the renowned person's life.

5. Burnout:

Burnout is a typical result of a constant quest for popularity, with people driving themselves to the edge of physical and profound fatigue.

The Model's Existence:

For models who accomplish popularity, the clouded side is a consistently present shadow, projecting its own extraordinary difficulties.

1. Extraordinary Media Concentration:

Well known models frequently persevere through extreme media examination, with everything they might do and appearance recorded in sensationalist newspapers and via online entertainment.

2. Assumption for Flawlessness:

The displaying business anticipates models, particularly renowned ones, to keep a picture of flawlessness, both apparently and conduct.

3. Contention and Rivalry:

Contention and rivalry among models can be furious, and notoriety escalates the serious idea of the business.

4. Brief Professions:

The demonstrating scene's passing nature implies that popularity can be fleeting, with models frequently wrestling with the truth of a post-distinction profession.

**5. Cultural Impact:

Well known models employ huge impact over cultural magnificence goals and principles, an obligation that can be both enabling and difficult.

Chapter Seven

The Impact of Diversity

Variety is a multi-layered idea that contacts practically every part of human existence. It isn't bound to a solitary space yet rather penetrates and impacts different circles, from culture and society to the work environment and the regular world. The effect of variety, whether as various foundations, viewpoints, or attributes, is significant and expansive, forming our encounters and molding our general surroundings in manners both unpretentious and obvious. This exposition digs into the mind boggling and complex elements of variety, looking at its effect on society, training, business, and the climate.

Society: An Embroidery of Contrasts

Society is an embroidery woven from the strings of individual contrasts, each strand adding to the mind boggling and lively texture that makes up our worldwide local area. Variety in the public eye envelops a large number of aspects, including however not restricted to race, nationality, orientation, religion, sexual direction, age, and financial status. These distinctions, while here and there a wellspring of strain and struggle, eventually make society rich and dynamic.

One of the most prompt and critical effects of variety in the public eye is the advancement of inclusivity and correspondence. At the point when people from assorted foundations are perceived and esteemed for their remarkable commitments, it encourages a climate wherein all individuals feel regarded and have equivalent open doors. Comprehensive social orders benefit from a more extensive scope of viewpoints, imagination, and critical thinking draws near, which, thusly, can prompt development and social advancement.

Variety can likewise be an impetus for social change. At the point when different gatherings meet up, they might challenge existing standards and biases. This can prompt the breakdown of generalizations and unfair practices, as well as the progression of additional fair regulations and arrangements. For instance, the Social liberties Development in the US, driven by assorted voices looking for racial equity, achieved huge authoritative changes that changed the scene of American culture.

Be that as it may, variety in the public eye isn't without its difficulties. Contrasts can some of the time lead to mistaken assumptions, clashes, and even brutality. These contentions might come from profoundly imbued predispositions or an absence of openness to different points of view. In such cases, schooling and exchange become fundamental apparatuses for tending to and conquering these difficulties.

Instruction: An Impetus for Understanding

Training assumes a critical part in molding how people see and explore variety. In an undeniably globalized world, schools and colleges are where youthful personalities first experience a mosaic of various societies, convictions, and foundations. The effect of variety in training is both significant and sweeping.

Variety in instructive settings enhances the opportunity for growth by presenting understudies to many points of view and perspectives. This openness energizes decisive reasoning and encourages social ability, as understudies figure out how to draw in with and value contrasts. Besides, it sets them up for the real factors of the labor force and a general public that is progressively interconnected.

Simultaneously, various instructive conditions can challenge generalizations and predispositions. At the point when understudies connect with peers from various foundations, they frequently find the shared traits that tight spot mankind together. Such associations can prompt more sympathetic, receptive, and socially touchy people.

Moreover, instructive establishments have an obligation to advance inclusivity and equivalent open doors. At the point when variety is reflected in workforce and staff, as well as in the educational program and showing materials, it sends a strong message that all voices are esteemed. This advantages understudies as well as adds to a more evenhanded society by separating hindrances to schooling and work for generally underestimated gatherings.

In any case, the instructive effect of variety isn't uniform across all establishments. Differences in instructive access and quality continue in many regions of the planet, and underestimated networks frequently face critical boundaries to getting quality training. These differences can propagate social imbalances and upset the full acknowledgment of the advantages of variety in schooling.

Business: Different Labor force, Upper hand

The business world has not been invulnerable to the effect of variety. As a matter of fact, variety in the working environment has acquired expanding consideration as additional organizations perceive the worth of a different labor force. The advantages of variety in business are various and reach out to the two workers and the association in general.

Various groups are known to be more creative and better at critical thinking. At the point when people from various foundations team up, they offer different viewpoints and encounters that would be useful. This variety of thought can prompt more clever fixes and items. Besides, it can upgrade an organization's capacity to adjust to changing business sector requests.

Variety can likewise further develop worker fulfillment and maintenance. A different and comprehensive workplace is bound to draw in top ability, as occupation searchers are progressively searching for work environments that mirror their qualities and convictions. Representatives in different associations frequently report higher work fulfillment since they feel esteemed and included.

Moreover, variety can be a wellspring of upper hand. Organizations that embrace variety are better prepared to comprehend and take care of a more extensive client base. This is especially significant in a globalized economy where organizations need to engage shoppers from different foundations. It can likewise assist with relieving chances related with mindless compliance and the homogenization of thoughts inside an association.

In any case, accomplishing and keeping up with variety in the working environment isn't without its difficulties. Making a comprehensive corporate culture requires exertion and responsibility. It requires tending to predispositions in recruiting, advancing, and pay rehearses. It likewise requires cultivating a climate where representatives have a solid sense of security to voice their viewpoints and contribute their extraordinary viewpoints.

The Climate: Biodiversity and Biological system Versatility

The effect of variety isn't bound to human culture and organizations; it stretches out to the regular world too. Biodiversity, the assortment of life on The planet, is a key part of our planet's wellbeing and flexibility. The perplexing snare of living things, from organisms to warm blooded animals, assumes basic parts in biological systems and impacts our personal satisfaction in manners that are frequently undervalued.

Biodiversity is fundamental for the soundness of environments. In assorted biological systems, various species can possess different natural specialties, which lessens rivalry for assets. This equilibrium guarantees the accessibility of fundamental administrations like fertilization, supplement cycling, and vermin control. Conversely, in less different biological systems, the departure of a solitary animal types can have significant gradually expanding influences, possibly prompting environment breakdown.

Moreover, biodiversity can be a wellspring of strength even with natural difficulties. Various biological systems are better prepared to endure unsettling influences, for example, environmental change or infection episodes, as various species might answer distinctively to these tensions. This strength is imperative for the general soundness of the planet and its capacity to help life.

Biodiversity likewise has substantial advantages for people. It furnishes us with food, medication, clean water, and different assets. A significant number of the plants and creatures we depend on for food and prosperity are important for the rich embroidery of life on The planet. Moreover, various biological systems can add to our psychological and close to home prosperity by offering open doors for entertainment, motivation, and profound association.

In spite of the basic significance of biodiversity, it is under danger. Human exercises, like deforestation, living space obliteration, over-exploitation of normal assets, and contamination, have prompted a sensational loss of animal groups and environments. The outcomes of this misfortune are broad and incorporate the interruption of environments, the disintegration of hereditary variety, and the potential for the spread of infections.

Interconnection: Where Aspects of Variety Combine

One of the most captivating parts of variety is the manner by which various components of variety cross and cross-over. The idea of interconnection recognizes that a singular's encounter of variety is molded by the transaction of different parts of their character. For instance, an individual's encounter as a lady of variety is molded by their orientation as well as by their race and nationality.

Diversity features the intricacy of human experience and highlights the significance of thinking about the full scope of a singular's attributes and encounters. It is an update that variety can't be diminished to a solitary aspect however is the consequence of a large number of elements that cooperate and impact each other.

Understanding and tending to diversity is fundamental in accomplishing genuine value and inclusivity. It requires perceiving that people might confront different layers of segregation and honor in light of different parts of their personality. For instance, a handicapped, transsexual individual might encounter extraordinary difficulties that vary from those looked by a non-crippled, cisgender individual. This acknowledgment is urgent in making arrangements and practices that are really comprehensive and evenhanded.

7.1. The Importance of Inclusivity in the Fashion Industry

The design business, once known for its eliteness and limited magnificence norms, is going through a significant change. Lately, there has been a developing acknowledgment of the significance of inclusivity in the design world. This shift is driven by different variables, including changing cultural mentalities, shopper interest for portrayal, and the business' acknowledgment of its monetary potential. In this article, we investigate the meaning of inclusivity in the style business, analyzing what it means for society, the business scene, and the people who take part in this powerful and persuasive area.

Society: Mirroring This present reality

Design isn't just about clothing; it's an impression of society's qualities, convictions, and character. Inclusivity in the design business is fundamental since it has the ability to shape how society sees itself as well as other people. At the point when the style world hugs variety in the entirety of its structures, it sends a strong message that individuals from different foundations are acknowledged as well as celebrated.

By and large, style has frequently propagated slender excellence principles that prohibit individuals who don't fit a specific shape. This rejection adversely affects people's confidence, self-perception, and generally speaking prosperity. Conversely, embracing inclusivity permits individuals to see themselves addressed in the media, on the runway, and in notices. This portrayal is enabling, as it lets individuals know that they have a place and that their novel credits are esteemed.

Inclusivity likewise has a more extensive cultural effect by testing and reshaping the manner in which society sees magnificence, personality, and the idea of "ordinary." It empowers a more comprehensive and tolerating society where individuals are passed judgment on less by their adjustment to conventional norms and more by their personality, gifts, and singularity. This shift adds to a more lenient and receptive society.

Moreover, design can possibly be a vehicle for social change. At the point when the business embraces inclusivity, it can carry significant issues to the bleeding edge and rock the boat. For example, the utilization of models of different sizes and body types has lighted conversations about body energy and the need to challenge the predominance of dietary issues and unreasonable excellence goals. Style can be an impetus for significant discoursed that affect society.

Nonetheless, the style business' excursion toward inclusivity isn't without its difficulties. While progress has been made, there is still quite far to go concerning portrayal. It's urgent for the business to guarantee that inclusivity is certainly not a simple pattern yet a supported responsibility, mirroring the different embroidery of society reliably.

Business Scene: A Developing Business sector

Inclusivity isn't just an issue of social obligation yet in addition an essential move for the style business according to a business point of view. The market for comprehensive style has filled fundamentally lately, and brands that embrace variety stand to financially benefit.

One critical part of this development is the expanded buying force of different buyer gatherings. As society turns out to be more different, customer interest for items that take care of different necessities and inclinations has developed. This shift has prompted an ascent in brands that focus on inclusivity, offering clothing lines and extras that take care of a wide scope of sizes, nationalities, sexes, and capacities. Subsequently, inclusivity isn't simply an ethical basic yet a monetary one, as brands that neglect to fulfill the needs of this developing business sector might end up in a difficult situation.

Moreover, embracing inclusivity can upgrade a brand's standing and picture. Buyers today are more aware of the qualities and morals of the brands they support. A guarantee to inclusivity can create positive advertising and client unwaveringness, as individuals are bound to help marks that line up with their qualities.

Inclusivity in the style business is additionally basic for drawing in and holding assorted ability. A more comprehensive working environment is probably going to be more inventive and better prepared to satisfy the needs of a different market. In that capacity, inclusivity is fundamental for enlisting and holding an imaginative and talented labor force, which is imperative for outcome in the cutthroat design scene.

Nonetheless, it is essential to perceive that the style business isn't resistant to allegations of performative inclusivity. A few brands have been censured for posturing, where variety and inclusivity are utilized as showcasing strategies with next to no certified obligation to foundational change. To genuinely profit from inclusivity, the style business should go past superficial changes and work towards cultivating a comprehensive culture and inventory network.

People: Strengthening and Self-Articulation

Inclusivity in the design business significantly affects people, as it engages them to articulate their thoughts genuinely and unhesitatingly. Style is a medium through which individuals convey their personality, and when it embraces inclusivity, it permits people to do as such unafraid of judgment or rejection.

For the people who have generally been minimized or underrepresented in the design world, inclusivity gives a feeling of approval and acknowledgment. At the point when they see models, creators, and commercials that address them, it sends a strong message that their personality and encounters are legitimate. This approval can help confidence and make a feeling of having a place.

Inclusivity in style likewise supports self-articulation and imagination. At the point when people are allowed to dress in a manner that mirrors their genuine selves, it advances a feeling of organization and command over their picture. This can be especially enabling for individuals who have felt compelled by cultural standards or magnificence guidelines.

Besides, inclusivity significantly affects psychological well-being and prosperity. At the point when people see themselves addressed emphatically in the media and style, it can decrease sensations of distance and uncertainty. It can likewise challenge the assimilated predispositions and negative self-discernments that can come about because of being assaulted with selective excellence beliefs.

Inclusivity in the design business can likewise prompt expanded vocation open doors for people from underestimated foundations. Creators, models, and experts from different nationalities, sexes, capacities, and body types get an opportunity to exhibit their gifts and add to the business. This can be both specifically satisfying and monetarily fulfilling, offering people a pathway to a satisfying and effective vocation.

Notwithstanding, there are difficulties that people face in exploring the design business, especially in its beginning phases of embracing inclusivity. Breaking into an industry that has been generally selective can be overwhelming, and people from minimized foundations might confront separation and inclination. Besides, people who decide to challenge customary standards might in any case experience cultural bias and backfire. Notwithstanding these difficulties, the developing help for inclusivity in the style world is bit by bit changing the scene, giving more open doors and acknowledgment.

The Street Ahead: A Guarantee to Inclusivity

Inclusivity in the design business is certainly not a passing pattern; it addresses a key change in the manner in which the business works and impacts society. Nonetheless, there is still a lot of work to be finished to guarantee that this shift is exhaustive and manageable.

One basic part of inclusivity is portrayal. The business should keep on pursuing different and exact portrayal in all angles, from runway models to publicizing efforts and positions of authority. It isn't sufficient to have one symbolic model from an underestimated bunch;

genuine inclusivity includes establishing a climate where different viewpoints are heard and esteemed.

Instruction and mindfulness are additionally fundamental. The style business should keep on teaching itself about the exceptional difficulties looked by changed gatherings and do whatever it may take to address those difficulties. This remembers advancing variety for configuration schools, encouraging a more comprehensive working environment culture, and making space for discourse about the effect of design on society.

Besides, inclusivity should stretch out past the surface and become imbued in the business' DNA. This implies taking on inclusivity as a promoting system as well as a guiding principle. Brands should coordinate inclusivity into their store network, from plan to creation to promoting. This incorporates utilizing different groups to guarantee that items take care of a great many requirements and inclinations.

The design business likewise plays a part to play in testing fundamental issues, for example, body disgracing, segregation, and natural maintainability. By utilizing its foundation to resolve these issues, the business can add to more extensive social change.

7.2. Stories of Diverse Contestants

In the domain of ability rivalries, the stage is much of the time set for enamoring stories that resound with crowds all over the planet. These accounts show some signs of life through the assorted candidates who take an interest, each with their exceptional foundations, battles, and desires. Whether it's a singing rivalry, a dance show, or some other ability grandstand, the people who step into the spotlight convey with them stories that move, challenge, and join us. This paper digs into the accounts of assorted challengers in the realm of ability contests and analyzes the effect of their excursions on both themselves and society.

The Force of Portrayal

Portrayal matters. At the point when challengers from different foundations partake in ability contests, they bring to the front stories that are frequently ignored or underrepresented in traditional press.

These accounts incorporate the battles of minimized networks, the victory over affliction, and the quest for dreams despite everything.

One strong part of portrayal is the perceivability it gives. Challengers who split away from customary standards old enough, orientation, identity, or capacity show the world that ability knows no limits. They rouse other people who might have confronted comparative difficulties or hindrances, demonstrating that defeating them and reach for their aspirations is conceivable.

For example, when a little kid from an underestimated local area grandstands her dance abilities on a broadcast contest, she exhibits her ability as well as fills in as a good example for other people who could have grown up with restricted open doors. Her process can motivate others to seek after their fantasies and put stock in their capacities, no matter what their experience.

Testing Generalizations

Ability contests likewise assume an essential part in testing generalizations. They separate assumptions about what people from assorted foundations can accomplish. For instance, a competitor with a the handicap crowd with a stunning presentation challenges the generalization that individuals with incapacities are restricted in their capacities.

These competitors show that they are characterized by their gifts and interests instead of their incapacities, and this rethinking can significantly affect cultural insights. It powers individuals to reconsider their predispositions and perceive the undiscovered capacity in people who have been customarily underrated or rejected.

Moreover, candidates who oppose orientation standards add to the continuous fight for orientation correspondence. A female drummer who wows the appointed authorities or a male ballet performer who nimbly makes that big appearance can motivate discussions about how orientation shouldn't limit one's quest for enthusiasm or achievement. These accounts accentuate the significance of splitting away from unbending orientation jobs and assumptions, opening the entryway for more prominent inclusivity and strengthening.

Defeating Misfortune

Numerous competitors in ability contests have confronted colossal difficulty in their lives. Whether it's experiencing childhood in destitution, managing segregation, or fighting individual difficulties, their accounts frequently reverberate profoundly with crowds. The persistence, strength, and assurance they show on the stage can be a wellspring of motivation for the individuals who are confronting their own battles.

These candidates become images of trust and strength, exhibiting that defeating difficulty through ability and difficult work is conceivable. Their accounts show that ability contests are tied in with winning an award as well as about figuring out how to transcend life's challenges and follow one's fantasies.

One strong model is the narrative of a youthful evacuee who, in spite of encountering the difficulties of dislodging, tracks down comfort and strength in singing. Their process represents the mending force of music and fills in as a sign of the flexibility that displaced people can have. It can prompt expanded mindfulness and sympathy for the difficulties looked by dislodged people around the world.

Various Societies and Customs

Ability rivalries frequently become a stage for the festival of different societies and customs. Challengers from various regions of the planet bring their one of a kind works of art and gifts to a worldwide stage. This variety isn't just an open door to feature the lavishness of human culture yet additionally to advance multifaceted comprehension and appreciation.

For example, a contender who plays out a customary dance from their country can acquaint watchers with the magnificence of that culture. It offers a chance for social trade, permitting individuals from assorted foundations to appreciate and gain from one another's practices.

The presence of different societies and customs in ability contests encourages a feeling of solidarity and association. That's what it exhibits, regardless of the distinctions in dialects, customs, and foundations, there are widespread feelings and encounters that associate individuals from everywhere the world.

Changing the Standards of Magnificence

The style and excellence principles sustained by the media have for some time been condemned for their eliteness. Be that as it may, ability rivalries are continuously changing the story by testing customary standards of magnificence. Competitors who don't fit the cliché picture of a model or entertainer feature that magnificence comes in different structures.

These competitors frequently address different body types, skin tones, and facial highlights, communicating something specific that excellence ought not be bound to a restricted arrangement of principles. Their presence helps in rethinking the idea of magnificence, advancing body energy, and empowering self-acknowledgment among watchers who might have felt distanced by conventional excellence beliefs.

Generally, ability rivalries offer a phase where challengers can embrace their uniqueness and act as heroes of self esteem and certainty. For some watchers, seeing people who look like them on the stage can be a wellspring of strengthening, giving them the certainty to embrace their own magnificence, paying little heed to cultural assumptions.

Inclusivity Past the Stage

While ability rivalries have taken huge steps in advancing inclusivity and variety, there is still a lot of work to be finished. Inclusivity ought not be restricted to the candidates who perform in front of an audience however ought to reach out to all parts of the creation, from the passing judgment on boards to the creation groups.

This includes guaranteeing that the making a decision about boards contain people from different foundations who can give balanced and fair evaluations of the hopefuls' exhibitions. A different passing judgment on board can likewise act as good examples for contenders and watchers the same.

Also, ability contests genuinely must know about social responsiveness and keep away from social apportionment. Competitors ought to be urged to commend their own societies and customs unafraid of distortion or inhumanity.

Inclusivity in ability rivalries ought to likewise reach out to the in the background ability. Creation groups, chiefs, choreographers, and beauticians ought to mirror different points of view and foundations. This guarantees that the end result is a genuine portrayal of the different gifts in front of an audience.

Besides, ability contests can additionally advance inclusivity by teaming up with associations that help underestimated networks. These joint efforts can assist with bringing issues to light of different social issues and give open doors to underrepresented people to partake.

The Effect of Virtual Entertainment

In the present computerized age, the effect of ability rivalries and the accounts of assorted hopefuls can stretch out past the stage. Online entertainment has turned into an amazing asset for candidates to interface with their crowds and offer their excursions, considerations, and encounters.

Competitors can utilize their virtual entertainment stages to bring issues to light about significant issues and draw in with their supporters in significant ways. They become advocates for social change, utilizing their accounts and voices to reveal insight into the difficulties looked by their networks or to help causes they are enthusiastic about.

Thusly, web-based entertainment permits crowds to connect all the more profoundly with challengers and their accounts. Watchers can offer help, commend their accomplishments, and become piece of a bigger local area that shares their qualities and desires. This interconnectedness intensifies the effect of inclusivity and takes into account more significant discourse and social change.

The Obligations of the Business

The style and media outlet holds a critical obligation in advancing inclusivity in ability rivalries. The business should effectively search out and sustain ability from different foundations and to guarantee that inclusivity is certainly not a symbolic signal yet a certified obligation to change.

One part of this responsibility is the advancement of variety in the choice of hopefuls. The business ought to effectively search out people from minimized networks and give them the help and assets expected to take part. This incorporates projecting a wide net for try-outs, offering preparing and mentorship, and setting out open doors for underrepresented ability.

Inclusivity ought to likewise be reflected in the organization of the creation groups and judges. Different voices ought to be addressed at each level to guarantee that the opposition is fair, deferential, and genuinely comprehensive.

Moreover, the business plays a part to play in forming the stories around the challengers. While it's critical to feature the special accounts of different competitors, decreasing them to their experiences or challenges is similarly urgent not. Challengers ought to be commended for their abilities and goals, not exclusively for their misfortune.

Besides, the business ought to effectively neutralize the propagation of generalizations and biases. This incorporates giving instruction and mindfulness projects to the two competitors and crowds to challenge inclinations and advance comprehension.

7.3. Creating a More Representative Fashion World

The universe of design has for quite some time been a domain of charm, inventiveness, and impact. However, for a long time, it has been related with selectiveness and an absence of variety, with an emphasis on a restricted scope of body types, nationalities, and foundations. In any case, lately, the style business has been gradually however consistently going through a change. There is a developing acknowledgment of the requirement for a more delegate and comprehensive design world, one that mirrors the variety of the worldwide populace and difficulties conventional standards. This paper investigates the significance of making a more delegate design industry, inspecting the effect on people, society, and the actual business.

Portrayal Matters

One of the essential standards basic the push for a more delegate style world is that portrayal matters. At the point when the style business highlights models, planners, and powerhouses who mirror the variety of society, it sends a strong message that magnificence and style are not restricted to a thin arrangement of norms. It enables people who have felt minimized, avoided, or underrated by customary magnificence beliefs to feel seen, esteemed, and acknowledged.

For example, when a style brand exhibits a larger size model wearing its most recent assortment, it shows that the brand is comprehensive as well as builds up the possibility that excellence exists in different structures. This portrayal can support the confidence of people who might have battled with self-perception issues or felt constrained to adjust to unreasonable magnificence norms.

Besides, portrayal challenges well established generalizations and inclinations. For instance, when models from various racial foundations are highlighted unmistakably in design crusades, it helps challenge racial predispositions and grow the extent of excellence. It lets individuals know that their social foundations are not snags to being viewed as gorgeous or in vogue, yet rather components that add to their uniqueness and allure.

Cultural Effect

The effect of a more delegate style industry stretches out past the runway and the pages of magazines. It impacts cultural insights and standards, reshaping the manner in which individuals view themselves as well as other people. Design fills in as an impression of cultural qualities and standards, and when it embraces variety, it can challenge and change cultural perspectives.

Inclusivity in the design world adds to a more lenient and receptive society. It stands up against generalizations and inclinations by featuring that magnificence and style are not bound to a solitary shape. It encourages a culture that values independence and celebrates contrasts, whether those distinctions relate to body size, nationality, orientation character, or incapacity.

Furthermore, a more delegate design world can be an impetus for more extensive social change. It carries significant issues to the very front and can light conversations about points like body energy, orientation balance, and the acknowledgment of individuals with handicaps. For instance, when a design brand projects a transsexual model in a conspicuous job, it advances inclusivity as well as difficulties assumptions about orientation and character.

Besides, portrayal in design can give good examples to underrepresented networks. At the point when people from different foundations see somebody who seems as though them on the runway or in a style crusade, it can move them to seek after their own fantasies, whether those fantasies are in design or some other field. These good examples can significantly affect the yearnings and confidence of people who have generally been underrepresented.

Comprehensive Style as an Industry Standard

The design business assumes a vital part in molding cultural standards of excellence and style. Thus, the business should start to lead the pack in making a more delegate and comprehensive style world. It is a domain where patterns are set and where choices about who is incorporated and who is prohibited have an enduring effect.

Inclusivity in style ought not be viewed as a specialty or a brief pattern however as a crucial industry standard. This standard ought to be reflected at each level, from the choice of models to the formation of assortments to the promoting of items.

One part of this standard is to projected models who address an assortment of body types, nationalities, sexes, and capacities. Style brands ought to put forth a functioning attempt to guarantee that their missions mirror the variety of their client base and society all in all. This variety ought not be restricted to incidental posturing yet ought to be a steady practice.

Besides, the business ought to energize and uphold creators from assorted foundations. A more delegate style world requires variety in the countenances highlighted as well as in the personalities behind the plans. By encouraging the gifts of creators from different social, racial, and orientation foundations, the business can offer new viewpoints and styles that enticement for a more extensive crowd.

Inclusivity ought to stretch out to the in the background ability also. Creation groups, beauticians, picture takers, and cosmetics specialists ought to likewise address a different scope of voices and points of view. This guarantees that the innovative approach is saturated with inclusivity beginning to end.

One more fundamental component of a more comprehensive design industry is the dismissal of correcting and unreasonable excellence guidelines. Brands ought to advance legitimacy by displaying unretouched pictures and accentuating that blemishes and uniqueness make individuals wonderful. This shift helps in supporting that flawlessness isn't the objective and that acting naturally is sufficient.

The Obligation of Media and Advertising

The media and showcasing areas of the style business are compelling diverts in advancing a more delegate design world. They shape public insights and inclinations, and accordingly, they convey the obligation of making content that mirrors the variety of society.

Inclusivity in design media includes the festival of people from all foundations, regardless old enough, size, orientation, or nationality. This implies that design magazines, promoting efforts, and network shows ought to effectively search out and highlight models and characters who address the full range of variety. At the point when design media underscores the magnificence and style of people who are not piece of the conventional style shape, it sends a strong message about the worthiness of variety.

Besides, design media ought to avoid utilizing modified or artificially glamorized pictures that mutilate reality and make ridiculous magnificence beliefs. This training can inconveniently affect individuals' confidence and self-perception. Genuineness ought to be valued over counterfeit flawlessness.

Inclusivity ought to likewise stretch out to the language and stories utilized in style media. It is fundamental to try not to advance destructive generalizations and inclinations. For example, terms that build up regrettable generalizations or advance segregation ought to be supplanted with more comprehensive and unbiased language.

Inclusivity and Computerized Media

The ascent of computerized media and virtual entertainment stages has additionally changed the style business and given a stage to under-represented voices and points of view. Advanced media permits people to make content and contact a group of people without depending on customary guardians. This has enabled people from different foundations to share their accounts and challenge laid out standards.

Virtual entertainment, specifically, has turned into an integral asset for advancing inclusivity in the design world. It permits people to draw in with brands and the business, setting their voices heard and their expectations for change known. Hashtags and online missions have carried significant issues to the cutting edge, driving the business to tune in and adjust.

Computerized media likewise empowers people to make their substance and construct a following. This is especially significant for the individuals who have felt minimized or rejected by the conventional style industry. Forces to be reckoned with from various foundations, whether they center around humble design, hefty size style, orientation variety, or social legacy, have found a stage where they can share their remarkable points of view and styles.

In addition, advanced media has made style more open. Online commercial centers and social business have democratized design, permitting people to find and buy clothing that lines up with their style and values, paying little mind to where they live or their actual capacities.

Style as a Problem solver

The design business can possibly act as a problem solver, with regards to individual style as well as in forming more extensive social stories. By embracing inclusivity, it can add to the destroying of hurtful generalizations and the advancement of a more evenhanded and tolerating society.

One of the key regions where design can have a huge effect is in testing magnificence goals. The business can reclassify the idea of magnificence by praising uniqueness and dismissing the oppression of customary principles. At the point when design brands and media feature a different scope of models and characters, they widen the skylines of magnificence and stress that there is nobody size-fits-all meaning of engaging quality.

Besides, style can challenge and change conventional orientation standards. By highlighting orientation nonconforming models and plans, it urges individuals to investigate and communicate their personalities in manners that overcome conventional presumption. It likewise communicates something specific that people ought not be compelled by society's orientation standards and that style is a method for self-articulation and freedom.

Chapter Eight

The Pursuit of Passion

Enthusiasm is a strong and extraordinary power that can possibly influence our lives, drive us higher than ever, and permeate our reality with significance and satisfaction. The serious energy and responsibility impels people to seek after their fantasies, find their gifts, and have a significant effect on the world. This paper dives into the quest for energy, investigating its importance, the difficulties it presents, and the prizes it offers in different aspects of life, from individual satisfaction to proficient achievement and cultural advancement.

The Embodiment of Enthusiasm

At its center, energy is an extraordinary and faithful excitement for something. The internal fire powers our interests and keeps us roused, even despite hindrances. Energy is profoundly private and can appear in different structures, whether it's an affection for craftsmanship, a pledge to a reason, a commitment to a calling, or a dedication to a side interest.

Energy frequently rises above simple interest; it is a calling, an occupation, or a deep rooted mission. It takes people jump up in the first part of the day, anxiously expect every day, and push their limits to accomplish their objectives. It's the wellspring of that charging flash according to the people who have tracked down their actual reason for living.

The quest for enthusiasm isn't about moment satisfaction; it's a long and frequently testing venture. It's tied in with perceiving the main thing to you, focusing on that pursuit, and determinedly devoting time, exertion, and assets to it. It's additionally about embracing the vulnerability and inescapable difficulties that accompany depending on your instinct.

Energy in Private Life

In private life, energy assumes a significant part in molding individual encounters and connections. It has the ability to encourage a feeling of character and individual satisfaction, enhancing one's existence with reason and euphoria. The quest for energy in private life frequently envelops leisure activities, imaginative undertakings, self-improvement, and connections.

Leisure activities and Interests: Many individuals track down their enthusiasm in leisure activities or interests beyond work. Whether it's painting, planting, playing an Instrument, or cooking, participating in these exercises can be a wellspring of individual delight and fulfillment. Side interests offer a departure from everyday schedules and give a feeling of achievement, whether it's finishing a difficult riddle or growing a lovely nursery.

Innovative Pursuits: The universe of inventiveness, including composing, craftsmanship, music, and that's just the beginning, frequently gives a material to energetic self-articulation. These inventive outlets permit people to share their inward universes, points of view, and feelings with others. Through imaginative undertakings, individuals can interface on a profound level, pass on significant messages, and leave an enduring effect.

Self-improvement and Prosperity: The quest for self-improvement and prosperity is one more region where energy becomes an integral factor. Whether it's investigating otherworldliness, rehearsing care, or embracing a wellbeing venture, the quest for a better and really satisfying life can be driven by a singular's enthusiasm for personal development. Energy frequently powers the devotion and tirelessness expected to accomplish individual objectives and in general prosperity.

Connections: Enthusiasm likewise assumes a critical part in close connections. The power of early fascination, which we generally allude to as "becoming hopelessly enamored," is driven by enthusiasm. The profound power unites people, frequently prompting deep rooted bonds. Keeping an enthusiastic association in a drawn out relationship requires exertion, understanding, and a common obligation to supporting the relationship.

The Difficulties of Chasing after Enthusiasm

The quest for enthusiasm isn't without its difficulties. It frequently includes venturing outside one's usual range of familiarity and facing hindrances that can test one's responsibility and flexibility. A portion of the normal difficulties include:

Cultural Assumptions: Society frequently forces assumptions on people, impacting their decisions and ways. Seeking after one's energy might struggle with customary standards or profession assumptions, prompting outer tensions and judgment. Conquering these cultural assumptions can challenge.

Monetary Contemplations: Purposeful ventures or flighty profession decisions may not necessarily in every case turn out a steady revenue. Monetary steadiness is a critical worry for some people, which can lead them to settle on decisions in view of financial security as opposed to their actual enthusiasm. Offsetting monetary security with one's enthusiasm can be a perplexing issue.

Chance and Vulnerability: The quest for enthusiasm frequently includes venturing into the obscure, which can threaten. The gamble of disappointment, vulnerability about the future, and the potential for mishaps can overwhelm. Beating the feeling of dread toward the obscure is a basic part of the excursion.

Adjusting Liabilities: Offsetting individual interests with life's liabilities, like work, family, and different responsibilities, can be a critical test. Setting aside opportunity and energy to put resources into one's enthusiasm while meeting different commitments calls for compelling using time productively and prioritization.

Analysis and Uncertainty: Chasing after one's enthusiasm might welcome analysis and uncertainty from others. Whether it's opposing relatives, suspicious companions, or cruel pundits, confronting pessimism and incredulity can cripple. Remaining consistent with one's enthusiasm notwithstanding outer wariness requires versatility.

Burnout: The extraordinary drive related with enthusiasm can now and again prompt burnout. People might propel themselves excessively hard, disregard taking care of oneself, and become overpowered. Finding a harmony among commitment and taking care of oneself is vital to supporting energy over the long haul.

In spite of these difficulties, the quest for energy is a fundamental excursion for some people. Driven by an internal calling forces them to rely on their instincts and have a significant effect on their daily routines and the existences of others.

Enthusiasm in Proficient Life

The quest for enthusiasm likewise assumes a critical part in the expert circle. It can direct vocation decisions, drive advancement, and lead to exceptional achievements. Energy in proficient life frequently includes getting a new line of work or vocation way that lines up with one's inclinations, values, and goals.

Vocation Decisions: Picking a vocation way determined by energy can prompt a seriously satisfying proficient life. Many individuals make fulfillment and progress by working in fields they are really energetic about. Whether it's a lifelong in medication, training, innovation, or human expression, the arrangement of energy and calling can be a strong impetus for self-awareness and accomplishment.

Development and Imagination: Enthusiasm energizes advancement and inventiveness in the working environment. At the point when people are energetic about their work, they are bound to contribute the time and exertion expected to investigate groundbreaking thoughts, foster inventive arrangements, and push the limits of their field. Enthusiastic experts frequently rouse their associates and drive hierarchical achievement.

Business: Business venture is a domain where enthusiasm frequently becomes the dominant focal point. Numerous business people start organizations driven by an enthusiasm for a specific item, administration, or cause. Their devotion to their vision fills the assurance expected to explore the difficulties and vulnerabilities of business.

Administration and Effect: Enthusiastic experts frequently become normal pioneers. Their excitement and responsibility motivate others, establishing a positive workplace and prompting significant achievements. Enthusiastic pioneers can drive positive change inside associations and businesses.

All consuming purpose Joining: The quest for enthusiasm frequently obscures the lines among work and individual life. Enthusiastic experts might find that their work doesn't feel like a weight; all things considered, it turns into a necessary piece of their life's motivation. Accomplishing a feeling of labor of love reconciliation can prompt more noteworthy generally fulfillment and prosperity.

The Crossing point of Individual and Expert Energy

For a few lucky people, individual enthusiasm and expert energy meet. This arrangement between what one is enthusiastic about actually and what one really does expertly can be groundbreaking. It permits people to get individual satisfaction from their work and carries a feeling of direction to their expert lives.

Imaginative Callings: Callings in artistic expression, including composing, painting, music, and performing, frequently empower people to consolidate their own and proficient interests. Imaginative experts find that their work and their own demeanor become profoundly entwined, bringing about a significant feeling of direction.

Social and Natural Causes: Numerous experts are driven by an enthusiasm for social or ecological causes. These people frequently work in philanthropic associations, backing gatherings, or corporate social obligation jobs where their expert endeavors line up with their own qualities and convictions.

Science and Exploration: Logical scientists and scholastics frequently experience major areas of strength for a between their own advantages and their expert work. This combination of energy can prompt earth shattering revelations and progressions in their fields.

Business venture: Business visionaries who start organizations established to their greatest advantage and interests experience a huge cross-over between their own and proficient lives. Their work turns into a sign of their most profound feelings and goals.

The Awards of Seeking after Enthusiasm

The quest for energy offers various prizes, both in private and expert life. These prizes reach out past private satisfaction and can emphatically influence society all in all.

Individual Satisfaction: Seeking after one's enthusiasm prompts a significant feeling of individual satisfaction. It offers a more profound comprehension of one's qualities, interests, and qualities. People who are enthusiastic about their interests frequently report more significant levels of happines.

8.1. The Driving Force Behind Each Model

The universe of displaying is a domain where excellence, style, and charm merge, enamoring the consideration of crowds all over the planet. Nonetheless, underneath the stunning outside, the design business is energized by the energy, assurance, and novel accounts of its models. Each model has a main impetus, a strong inspiration that moves them into the spotlight and keeps them there. This article investigates the different and frequently motivating main impetuses behind models, revealing insight into the individual stories that shape their vocations and impact the design world.

A Complex Industry

The demonstrating business is a multi-layered substance, incorporating a large number of classes, from high style and publication to business and hefty size displaying. Every classification draws in people with their particular stories, foundations, and inspirations.

High Style Models: High design models are many times the encapsulation of marvelousness, swaggering down runways in creator articles of clothing and gracing the pages of renowned design magazines. For some, the main impetus behind turning into a high style model is the charm of creative articulation and the chance to work with prestigious originators, photographic artists, and cosmetics craftsmen. They see displaying as a type of craftsmanship and self-articulation, a material whereupon they can project their extraordinary style and vision.

Article Models: Publication models are the countenances behind design article spreads in magazines and promotion crusades. Their main impetus is many times a firmly established enthusiasm for narrating through symbolism. They consider displaying to be a method for conveying feelings, stories, and ideas. Publication models are driven by their longing to recount to a visual story that charms and rouses.

Business Models: Business models are the appealing essences of promoting efforts, highlighted in everything from item ads to way of life shots. Their main thrust is the amazing chance to address and associate with ordinary customers. They consider themselves to be channels for appealing and open magnificence. They want to motivate people to relate to the items and encounters they advance.

Larger Size Models: Hefty size models have reshaped the business by upholding for body inspiration and inclusivity. Their main thrust frequently comes from individual encounters with self-perception issues and the longing to challenge cultural excellence principles. They see themselves as diplomats of self-acknowledgment and certainty, motivating others to embrace their bodies as they are.

Runway Models: Runway models are known for their balance and presence on the catwalk. Their main thrust is the excitement of playing out, the potential chance to epitomize the vision of a planner, and the opportunity to enamor a group of people. Runway models are spurred by the invigoration of the live show, the extraordinary force of design, and the possibility of having an enduring impression.

Wellness and Wellbeing Models: Wellness and wellbeing models are in many cases driven by an enthusiasm for health and a commitment to actual wellness. Their inspiration is attached in rousing others to carry on with better existences. They see themselves as good examples, empowering people to focus on their wellbeing and prosperity.

Imaginative and Cutting edge Models: Creative and vanguard models are attracted to the unpredictable and the exploratory. Their main impetus is the potential chance to push the limits of conventional magnificence and style. They consider themselves to be craftsmen, involving their bodies as materials to make cutting edge articulations and incite thought.

The Excursion of Goal

Each model's process starts with a flash of goal. Whether it's the fantasy about strolling the world's most lofty runways, gracing the pages of top design magazines, or being essential for historic missions, yearning is the impetus that gets the demonstrating vocation under way.

For some, this yearning emerges from early openness to the universe of style and excellence. As a youngster, they could have wondered about reflexive design magazines, watched runway shows on TV, or respected the polish of their #1 models. These early impacts act as a setting for their fantasies.

The way to turning into a model is frequently set apart by commitment and difficult work. It includes organizing, fostering a portfolio, going to projecting calls, and frequently confronting dismissal. Models are persistently refining their abilities and their picture, whether it's idealizing their runway walk, rehearsing their appearances, or keeping up with their physical make-up.

This excursion is interspersed by critical achievements, from handling the main displaying gig to marking with an esteemed organization. Every accomplishment reaffirms the model's responsibility and drives them further along their way.

The Force of Self-Articulation

At the core of many models' main thrust is the force of self-articulation. Demonstrating gives a remarkable stage to people to put themselves out there, their style, and their inventive vision. It permits them to become living materials, exemplifying the plans, feelings, and stories woven into each photoshoot or runway show.

Models frequently view themselves as craftsmen, and their bodies as instruments for making and conveying excellence. They track down satisfaction in the capacity to impart thoughts, feelings, and stories through their postures, articulations, and developments. They consider demonstrating to be a mode for narrating, a visual language that rises above words and resounds with crowds.

For high style and publication models, the runway and the camera focal point become their stage, where they can change into characters and personas, conveying the embodiment of a style planner's assortment or a picture taker's vision.

The force of self-articulation additionally stretches out to advancing individual convictions and values. Many models utilize their perceivability to advocate for social, ecological, and wellbeing related causes. They influence their public picture to bring issues to light and move positive change.

Breaking Hindrances and Moving Ideal models

Lately, the displaying business has encountered a critical shift toward inclusivity, body inspiration, and variety. Models who have been at the front of this change frequently have a main thrust established in breaking obstructions and testing customary excellence guidelines.

Larger size models, for instance, are much of the time persuaded by private encounters with self-perception issues. They see their job as groundbreaking, meaning to rethink magnificence guidelines and advance self-acknowledgment. By embracing their bodies as they are and supporting for inclusivity, they rouse people, all things considered, to adore and commend their novel magnificence.

Additionally, models of different ethnic foundations consider their vocations to be a potential chance to address and praise their legacy. They invest heavily in being representatives of social variety and provoking the business to be more comprehensive.

The business' change likewise stretches out to progress in years variety, with models of fluctuating age bunches testing age-related generalizations. They view themselves as rethinking ideas of magnificence and showing that style and moxy have no age limits.

The Job of Mentorship and Motivation

Many models credit their excursion to the mentorship and motivation they get from the individuals who have prepared. Laid out models frequently encourage yearning models, offering direction, guidance, and important associations.

These mentorships assume an essential part in sustaining and forming the professions of arising ability. Coaches give bits of knowledge into the business, share their encounters, and proposition support during the difficulties of the demonstrating scene.

Motivation additionally comes from notable figures in the business. Models might admire the individuals who have made incredible progress and impact, seeing them as good examples. The accomplishments of these famous figures act as a wellspring of inspiration and verification that their fantasies are feasible.

The Adventure of the Runway

For runway models, the main impetus frequently lies in the adventure of performing on the world's most lofty catwalks. The runway is the stage where models show some major signs of life, and their masterfulness is on full presentation.

The valuable chance to epitomize the vision of an eminent planner and charm a group of people is a strong inspiration. The runway permits models to feature their abilities, balance, and presence, having an enduring impression with each step they take. The fervor of live shows, the energy of the crowd, and the groundbreaking force of style join to make a remarkable and thrilling experience.

Runway models likewise track down motivation in the inventive strategy of rejuvenating a planner's vision. They consider themselves to be a critical component in the introduction of an assortment, assuming an essential part in conveying the originator's story and creative articulation.

The Quest for Self-awareness

For some models, the main thrust goes past the spotlight and the charm. They view demonstrating as a way to self-improvement and self-revelation. The business gives a stage to foster fearlessness, flexibility, and versatility.

Models frequently find that the requests of their calling push them to investigate their limits and advancement their usual ranges of familiarity. Confronting dismissal, analysis, and the afflictions of the business assists them with fostering a toughness and a solid feeling of assurance.

The openness to different encounters, individuals, and societies likewise cultivates self-awareness. Models frequently travel to different areas for photoshoots and shows, drenching themselves in various conditions and drawing in with individuals from varying backgrounds.

8.2. Sacrifices and Commitment

Chasing achievement and the acknowledgment of our objectives and dreams, we frequently experience the twin partners of penances and responsibility. These two ideas are profoundly interlaced, shaping the actual texture of the human experience. Penances address the value we will pay to accomplish our yearnings, while responsibility is the relentless commitment to our targets. This paper dives into the mind boggling connection among penances and responsibility, investigating how they shape our own and proficient lives, the difficulties they present, and the significant prizes they offer.

The Idea of Penances

Penances are the concessions we make chasing a more prominent great, be it individual or expert. They can take different structures, including the surrender of time, energy, solace, assets, and, surprisingly, individual cravings. The substance of penances lies in our ability to do without prompt satisfaction for long haul objectives.

Time Penances: Time is a limited asset, and distributing it to one pursuit frequently implies redirecting it from others. Forfeiting time can appear as committing extended periods to work, instruction, or a specific task while decreasing relaxation exercises and individual time. It can likewise include being away from friends and family or passing up get-togethers.

Energy and Exertion Penances: Accomplishing significant objectives requires impressive exertion and commitment. This frequently involves exhausting physical and mental energy, at times stretching one's boundaries to achieve undertakings and defeat difficulties.

Safe place Penances: Safe places address the natural and places of refuge in our lives. Forfeiting one's usual range of familiarity implies embracing distress, hazard, and vulnerability in quest for development and accomplishment. It might include taking on new obligations, confronting fears, or adjusting to change.

Asset Penances: Monetary ventures, whether in schooling, business, or self-improvement, are a typical type of penance. Assets like cash, gear, or materials are focused on an endeavor, with the assumption for future returns.

Individual Longings and Aspirations: Individual penances can likewise reach out to deferring or changing individual cravings and desires. For instance, one could concede individual dreams to help the desires of friends and family, like family or accomplices.

Penances are not intrinsically regrettable; they are fundamental parts of progress and accomplishment. They imply an eagerness to focus on long haul satisfaction over prompt delight. Basically, penances are an interest from now on, a cognizant choice to distribute assets and endeavors toward an ideal result.

The Job of Responsibility

Responsibility is the unflinching devotion and take steps to seek after a specific goal, frequently despite snags and difficulties. The main thrust supports people on their picked way. Responsibility goes past simple interest; it exemplifies a significant feeling of direction and assurance.

Individual Responsibility: In private life, responsibility can be coordinated toward different objectives, including self-awareness, connections, or wellbeing and prosperity. Individual responsibility frequently includes setting explicit targets and making a reliable move to accomplish them. It can appear as a pledge to wellness, mastering another expertise, or fortifying a bond with a friend or family member.

Proficient Responsibility: In the expert domain, responsibility assumes a urgent part in vocation achievement. It is the commitment to a picked field, occupation, or task, described by difficult work, determination, and the quest for greatness. Proficient responsibility drives people to ceaselessly work on their abilities, comply with time constraints, and take on difficulties.

Obligation to a Reason: Numerous people are profoundly dedicated to social, ecological, or compassionate causes. This sort of responsibility includes pushing for change, bringing issues to light, and making unmistakable moves to help the reason. Obligation to a reason frequently rouses aggregate endeavors and achieves positive change.

Obligation to Connections: Solid and enduring connections are based on responsibility. Obligation to an accomplice, family, or companionship includes financial planning time, exertion, and profound energy to support and support the relationship. It incorporates a readiness to defeat clashes and difficulties together.

Responsibility can be communicated through constancy, versatility, and a refusal to surrender even with misfortunes. It is the undaunted faith in the worth of one's objectives and the assurance to own them to completion.

The Advantageous Relationship

Penances and responsibility are inseparably connected, framing a cooperative relationship. Responsibility frequently requires penances, as people apportion their assets and endeavors to understand their objectives. On the other hand, the penances made address the encapsulation of responsibility, as they mirror a profound devotion to accomplishing explicit targets.

Penances as an Indication of Responsibility: When people are focused on an objective, they are more able to make penances to accomplish it. This responsibility instills penances with reason and importance. For instance, somebody focused on a vocation may readily put time and exertion in training and expert turn of events, even at the expense of individual recreation.

Responsibility Energizes Penances: chasing a significant objective, the obligation to accomplishing it gives the inspiration to make penances. The strength of responsibility can engage people to get through difficulties, push through challenges, and pursue difficult decisions that could some way or another appear to be outlandish.

The transaction among penances and responsibility likewise fills in as a check of the meaning of the objective. The more noteworthy the responsibility, the more significant the penances are probably going to be, mirroring the significance and profundity of one's devotion.

Difficulties and Obstructions

The way of penances and responsibility isn't without its difficulties and obstructions. These hardships can test the purpose of people and require flexibility and assurance to survive.

Adjusting Needs: Adjusting individual, expert, and social needs can be a huge test. Obligation to one everyday issue could request penances in another. The test lies in successfully overseeing and dispensing assets and time.

Burnout: The tenacious quest for an objective can prompt physical and close to home burnout. The drive to make forfeits and keep up with elevated degrees of responsibility can, on occasion, come at the expense of one's prosperity. Staying balanced requires mindfulness, taking care of oneself, and the capacity to define limits.

Flexibility Despite Misfortunes: Responsibility frequently includes confronting difficulties and deterrents. How people answer these moves is a demonstration of their flexibility. Keeping up with responsibility through misfortune requires an undaunted confidence in the objective and an eagerness to adjust and gain from difficulties.

Remaining Consistent with Values: Remaining focused on an objective frequently requires remaining consistent with one's qualities and standards. It tends to be trying to stick to one's ethical compass, particularly in circumstances where penances could think twice about guidelines.

Managing Vulnerability: The quest for long haul objectives might involve confronting vulnerability and chance. Responsibility requires exploring uncertainty and settling on choices with a fragmented image representing things to come. It very well may be agitating, however it is a necessary piece of the excursion.

Conquering these provokes and impediments is a demonstration of the strength of responsibility. It requires a profound confidence in the worth of the objective, a readiness to adjust and learn, and the capacity to drive forward through difficulty.

The Significant Compensations of Penances and Responsibility

The way of penances and responsibility isn't without its prizes. The significant feeling of achievement and self-awareness that people experience frequently makes the excursion beneficial. The prizes stretch out to individual satisfaction, proficient achievement, and the positive effect on society.

Self-awareness: Responsibility and forfeits frequently lead to self-awareness. They challenge people to push their limits, foster new abilities, and gain a more profound comprehension of themselves. The excursion encourages versatility, flexibility, and an uplifted identity mindfulness.

Proficient Achievement: In the expert domain, responsibility is a vital driver of progress. The penances made to additional one's vocation frequently bring about accomplishments, acknowledgment, and professional success. Obligation to greatness and expert advancement makes ready for satisfying and remunerating vocations.

Accomplishing Significant Objectives: Responsibility and penances are the venturing stones to accomplishing significant and long haul objectives. They empower people to change their fantasies into the real world, whether in the fields of training, vocation, or individual desires.

Positive Effect on Society: Obligation to causes and social issues has the ability to impact positive change in the public eye. People who advocate for change and contribute their time, exertion, and assets in resolving cultural issues can have an enduring effect. Their responsibility can move others to join the reason, bringing about aggregate endeavors for everyone's benefit.

Extending Connections: In private life, obligation to connections frequently prompts further associations and enduring bonds. The eagerness to make forfeits and put resources into the development of a relationship can bring about getting through organizations and a solid emotionally supportive network.

Satisfaction of Individual Qualities: Remaining consistent with one's qualities and standards despite penances can prompt a significant feeling of satisfaction. This arrangement with one's center convictions is a demonstration of the strength of responsibility and its capacity to keep up with honesty.

The awards of penances and responsibility stretch out to the satisfaction of individual dreams, the advancement of society, and the getting through development of people. They are a demonstration of the persevering through force of commitment .

8.3. The Endless Pursuit of a Dream

The quest for a fantasy is an immortal and all inclusive undertaking that rises above topographical limits, societies, and ages. It is a characteristic piece of the human experience, energized by the yearnings, interests, and wants that dwell profound inside us. Whether it's the fantasy about accomplishing individual objectives, adding to society, or leaving an enduring inheritance, the quest for a fantasy is an excursion that characterizes our lives and shapes our fates. This paper investigates the substance of the interminable quest for a fantasy, the main thrusts behind it, the difficulties it presents, and the groundbreaking power it holds.

The Idea of Dreams

Dreams are the striking imaginings of a superior future, a dream of what could be. They take on assorted frames and can envelop individual, proficient, or cultural yearnings. Dreams might incorporate accomplishing scholastic greatness, succeeding in a specific field, beginning a family, encouraging social change, or making a masterpiece. The consistent idea among all fantasies is the faith in the chance of change, development, and satisfaction.

Individual Dreams: These fantasies are focused on individual desires and self-acknowledgment. Individual dreams frequently rotate around accomplishments, self-awareness, and bliss. They can include objectives like venturing to the far corners of the planet, turning into a gifted performer, or discovering a genuine sense of harmony.

Proficient Dreams: Proficient dreams are connected with one's profession and desires. These fantasies might include succeeding in a specific calling, beginning an effective business, or having a tremendous effect in one's field. The quest for proficient dreams is many times driven by a craving for acknowledgment, monetary achievement, and the chance to make a significant commitment.

Cultural Dreams: A few dreams reach out past the individual and are devoted to making positive change in the public eye. These fantasies incorporate a large number of tries, from supporting for civil rights and natural protection to advocating training and medical care access for all. They are many times inspired by a promise to making the world a superior spot.

Imaginative and Inventive Dreams: Imaginative and inventive dreams are focused on creative articulation and development. These fantasies incorporate many creative pursuits, from composing a novel, painting a work of art, forming music, or arranging a dance. They are much of the time portrayed by a profound energy for innovative articulation.

The quest for a fantasy is a profoundly private undertaking. Dreams are the results of our special encounters, values, and desires. They address an impression of our deepest longings and a dream representing things to come we wish to make.

The Main impetuses Behind Dreams

The quest for a fantasy is an excursion that requires resolute responsibility and assurance. The main thrusts behind dreams are the impetuses that push people forward and support them on this groundbreaking way.

Energy: Enthusiasm is the serious and resolute love for one's fantasy. The fuel lights the quest for a fantasy and keeps the fire consuming. Energy implants existence with reason, excitement, and energy. It drives people to contribute time, exertion, and assets in the acknowledgment of their fantasies.

Trust: Trust is the conviction that the fantasy is feasible and that a more promising time to come is conceivable. The directing light motivates people to beat deterrents and difficulties. Trust gives the flexibility to climate mishaps and proceed with the excursion with idealism.

Assurance: Assurance is the immovable obligation to accomplishing the fantasy, no matter what the troubles experienced. The inward purpose pushes people to continue notwithstanding affliction and vulnerability. Assurance enables people to make a reliable move towards their objectives.

Vision: Vision is the reasonable image of the fantasy and its possible results. It gives an internal compass and motivation, directing people in their interest. A distinctive and clear cut vision is a wellspring of motivation, rousing people to work steadily toward their objectives.

Self-Conviction: Self-conviction is the immovable trust in one's capacities and ability to accomplish the fantasy. The inward strength counters self-uncertainty and dread. Self-conviction enables people to face challenges, embrace difficulties, and endure in their interest.

Versatility: Flexibility is the capacity to quickly return from misfortunes and adjust to evolving conditions. It is the ability to endure through misfortune and arise more grounded. Flexibility guarantees that difficulties experienced chasing a fantasy don't become detours.

The main impetuses behind dreams are profoundly interconnected and frequently support one another. Enthusiasm, trust, assurance, vision, self-conviction, and versatility work pair to give the inspiration and strength expected to support the excursion of seeking after a fantasy.

The Difficulties of Seeking after a Fantasy

The quest for a fantasy isn't without its difficulties and hindrances. The excursion is frequently set apart by hardships and difficulties that test one's purpose and assurance. These difficulties can take different structures, and the capacity to explore them is a demonstration of the strength of the visionary.

Vulnerability: Chasing after a fantasy frequently includes venturing into the unexplored world. Vulnerability can appear as uncertainty about the achievability of the fantasy, anxiety about the future, or worries about expected chances. Beating vulnerability requires areas of strength for an of trust and self-conviction.

Misfortunes: Difficulties are an integral part of the excursion. They might come as disappointments, dismissals, or unforeseen snags. The capacity to bounce back from difficulties and use them as venturing stones toward the fantasy is pivotal.

Penances: Chasing after a fantasy might require penances in different parts of life, like time, assets, individual solace, and recreation. Penances can represent a test as people should gauge the compromises between prompt delight and long haul objectives.

Analysis and Uncertainty: Outside analysis and uncertainty from others can discourage. It might come as distrust, pessimism, or demoralization. Dealing with analysis and uncertainty includes keeping up with self-conviction and flexibility despite cynics.

Conquering Dread: Anxiety toward the obscure, apprehension about disappointment, and feeling of dread toward dismissal are normal obstructions. Standing up to and defeating dread is a basic piece of seeking after a fantasy. It requires fortitude and a pledge to venturing outside one's usual range of familiarity.

Balance: Finding a harmony between the quest for a fantasy and other life obligations can challenge. People should shuffle their desires with individual and expert responsibilities. Finding some kind of harmony is indispensable to guarantee generally prosperity.

Diligence: Steadiness is the capacity to proceed with the excursion in any event, when progress is slow or achievement appears to be far off. It is a trial of one's assurance and resolve. Persistence requires the perseverance to continue onward, in any event, when the way is testing.

Each challenge experienced on the way to seeking after a fantasy is a chance for development and learning. It is through defeating these difficulties that people foster versatility, flexibility, and the solidarity to persevere in their excursion.

The Groundbreaking Force of Dreams

The quest for a fantasy is a groundbreaking excursion that shapes people and society in significant ways. It has the ability to achieve self-awareness, positive change, and enduring effect.

Self-awareness: The quest for a fantasy encourages self-awareness and improvement. It moves people to extend their points of view, master new abilities, and defeat restrictions. It energizes self-disclosure and a profound comprehension of one's capacities and potential.

Positive Change: Dreams frequently lead to positive change, both in people's lives and in the public arena. Chasing after a fantasy can bring about imaginative arrangements, social advancement, and progressions in different fields. It can possibly drive change, rock the boat, and motivate others to follow after accordingly.

Flexibility and Versatility: The excursion of chasing after a fantasy fabricates strength and versatility. People figure out how to return quickly from mishaps, embrace change, and foster the capacity to flourish in various conditions. This flexibility stretches out past the quest for the fantasy and impacts different parts of life.

Motivation and Inspiration: The quest for a fantasy fills in as a wellspring of motivation for other people. At the point when people observer the commitment, enthusiasm, and assurance of visionaries, they are propelled to seek after their own yearnings. Dreams have a gradually expanding influence, moving a pattern of positive activity.

Inheritance and Effect: The quest for a fantasy can prompt an enduring heritage and effect. The accomplishments and commitments made chasing a fantasy make an imprint on society and people in the future. It is a demonstration of the getting through force of responsibility and yearning.

Instances of Perpetual Quest for Dreams

To show the getting through quest for dreams, it is important to investigate genuine instances of people who have resolutely endeavored to accomplish their goals. These models length various fields, each exhibiting the groundbreaking force of resolute responsibility.

Thomas Edison: Thomas Edison, the creator of the phonograph and the pragmatic electric light, represents the persevering quest for a fantasy. Regardless of confronting various disappointments and misfortunes as he continued looking for pivotal developments, Edison persevered. His obligation to development and enduring assurance prompted more than 1,000 licenses and pivotal commitments to the area of innovation.

Martin Luther Ruler Jr.: Dr. Martin Luther Ruler Jr. committed his life to the fantasy of racial fairness and social equality. He supported the reason for peaceful dissent and social change, confronting analysis, dangers, and detainment. Dr. Lord's obligation to the fantasy of correspondence enlivened a development that reshaped American culture and prompted.